19.50

D0152259

TOWARD A
HUMANITARIAN DIPLOMACY

TOWARD A HUMANITARIAN DIPLOMACY

A Primer for Policy

Edited by
Tom J. Farer

New York University Press. New York *and* London

For
Vladimir and Florence

Contents

Introduction

In the presidential campaign of 1976, marked, as usual, by a struggle to dominate the political center more by obscuring than defining policy conflicts, one of the few things Jimmy Carter decisively committed himself to was a new deal on human rights. Even a commitment more tempered than Carter's would have excited those like myself who felt that during the preceding decade this nation had strayed very far from its high if sometimes largely rhetorical ideals. For his arrival signaled the departure of Henry Kissinger, that cynical, ruthless child of Europe who for eight years had dominated American diplomacy. Carter's coming inevitably raised real hopes, leavened, however, by doubt whether a political and economic system organized like ours would tolerate the kinds of policy initiatives required for the effective promotion of human rights in other nations.

The precarious nature of race relations in the United States, for instance, would limit the executive's capacity to pressure the white enclaves of southern Africa. The reflexive hostility of most Americans to socialist, much less Marxist, political movements and their hardly diminished bipolar view of international politics constituted a second obstacle, one endowed with great force and global relevance. Public opinion would doubtless embrace tough initiatives on behalf of political prisoners in Cuba. But how would it react to the withdrawal of support from anticommunist regimes committed to a kind of capitalism? By force of precedent such regimes were friends, if not formal allies. And by virtue of their long association with the United States, they had accumulated the power to penetrate and significantly to influence the American political process.

Finally, hope and indeed desire for a new direction in the foreign policy of the United States was inevitably qualified by concern for the issue of peace. No active human-rights policy could ignore delinquencies committed by the Soviet Union and its satellites. But bringing human-rights issues to bear on the Soviet Union clashed harshly with the politics of cooperation because, as Stanley Hoffman has noted, raising the issue "touches on the very foundations of a regime, on its sources and exercise of power, on its links to its citizens or subjects."[1] Cooperation in arms control and other issues can be based on considerations of a complementary and balanced self-interest that bear no obvious relationship to differences over human rights. However, in an area such as arms control, much less limited disarmament, the parties need a measure of mutual confidence to overcome the inevitable, albeit, small risks and uncertainties which no written agreement can wholly eliminate. Since the Soviet Union was likely to construe United States condemnation of its domestic policies as a provocative challenge to fundamental interests, the human-rights issue could, conceivably, brake the momentum of arms control negotiations.

Seen in three-year retrospect, the obstacles to an active and relatively consistent human-rights diplomacy have proved every bit as formidable as the greater skeptics had anticipated. A centrist president instinctively flinches from challenges to conventional wisdom and established institutions. No institution is more established than corporate enterprise, just as there is no wisdom more solidly conventional among the stalwarts of the foreign policy community than the notion that the free movement of goods and money is a Good Thing. So it was hardly astonishing when Carter, early in his administration, ruled out restraints on private enterprise as a means for defending human rights. True to his word, Carter subsequently resisted a trade embargo against Idi Amin, only to be hauled into it by a determined Congress.

The electorate's and the media's manichaean view of foreign relations—which equates every new regime making Marxist noises with a Soviet victory—has played an erratic role in administration policy, its salience varying significantly with geographic proximity. In southern Africa, neither Soviet aid to Nkomo nor Mr. Mugabe's socialist-sounding dicta deterred the administration from its stated conviction that any tolerable Rhodesian solution must include the Patriotic Front. But in Nicaragua, the administration's fear of Marxist elements among the Sandinista guerrillas produced a policy reeking with hostility to the insurrectionists and thus prolonged the ineffable Somoza's reign. Equally flawed, by the standards of a humanitarian diplomacy, was the president's personal embrace of the Iranian Shah, before the torrents of revolution swept him into exile.

The Carter administration's calculus of strategic interests linked to the competitive relations between the United States and the Soviet Union muted criticism of authoritarian governments in the Philippines and South Korea, two countries where, unlike Iran, the democratic alternative to tyranny is reasonably well defined. Whether in a few years the United States government will once again be surprised by the overthrow of seemingly stable regimes and will then confront political leaders made hostile by an awareness of the collusion of the United States with their predecessors, only the clairvoyant will confidently predict. But surely even those policy-makers endowed with pedestrian foresight should be moved by the Iranian experience to open channels to dissident groups while reducing the excessive cordiality of their relations with anti-democratic incumbents. Those relations require nothing more than a dry, businesslike association limited to areas of exigent national interest.

Persons infused with excessive hope by Carter's evident if labored sincerity and the 1976 electorate's possibly whimsical romance with humanity are disappointed by his first-term performance. Such optimists carry around images of Carter preaching while Nicaragua burns or waltzing in the New Year with the Shah. Certainly a leftwing democrat would have done more. But such a man could not have been elected in 1976. The center was as far left as the system would move.

When Carter assumed office, in the southern part of that Free World conjured into existence by Cold War publicists enemies of freedom swaggered around bellowing contempt for human rights. Fascists or, as some prefer, corporatists seemed to pour out of the Latin American and other closets where they had been quietly nesting since the humiliating defeat of World War II. Throughout most of the noncommunist third world advocates of democracy appeared hard-pressed in eroding defensive positions. If he accomplished nothing else, through his consistent rhetoric and erratic initiatives Jimmy Carter turned the ideological tide.

I have no hesitation in crediting Carter for bringing about real electoral change in the Dominican Republic and the promise of democratic government in Ecuador, Peru, Bolivia, and, perhaps, eventually in Brazil. Nor do I question the judgement attributed to Kissinger and others that Carter's championing of human rights emboldened the Iranian Shah's opponents as it restrained the Shah's inclination towards an annihilating repression. And for all its depressing equivocation, the administration's withdrawal of support for the Somoza dynasty plainly encouraged the Nicaraguan people's decision to stand up.

Human-rights advocates will recall and honor those achievements. They will also recall the prudential advantages springing from the administration's relative sensitivity to the humanitarian dimension of other issues. By recognizing a measure of validity in Palestinian claims to autonomy, the United States could more effectively broker an Israeli-Egyptian settlement. And by tilting away from the whites of southern Africa, the United States shored up relations with Nigeria and enhanced its diminished influence in international forums.

So let us be fair. Placed beside the highest hopes of the human-rights movement, Jimmy Carter is a modest figure. In the history books yet to be written, however, he might come to seem much greater, for historians do not measure a President against dreamy ideals. Rather they look to the achievements of his predecessors. Carter surpasses that standard with something to spare. So, at any rate, it seems to this observer.

The essays in this volume are designed to help other spectators form their own conclusions. Between them, Farer and Vogelgesang sketch the opportunities and obstacles that confronted Carter and will continue to influence the policies of his or any successor administration. The case studies test and in varying degrees illustrate the preceding essays' generalizations about the margin where history offers scope for policy.

Many other cases that have engaged Administration concern—for example, Argentina, Brazil, Ethiopia, Indonesia—might, of course, have served the same purpose. Each instance has its own fascination without necessarily offering additional insights. The three cases chosen do illustrate, at least as well as any set of plausible alternatives, both the difficulties and opportunities which attend a humanitarian diplomacy.

In each case the United States had, or at least was widely thought to have had, both important interests and significant influence. But the precise nature of those interests, the best means for safeguarding them, the real extent of American influence, and the possibility of injurious retaliation by the target government were and remain controversial issues. Equally controversial in the cases of Iran and South Korea was the relative severity of the violations—in part a question of fact, in part a question of criteria. Even in the case of South Africa one hears voices questioning whether the delinquencies it practices are so grave as to justify the employment of serious political and economic coercion to force sweeping social change.

John de St. Jorre explicitly faces this issue and argues, I think persuasively, that South Africa represents a peculiarly egregious deviation from minimal, global standards of decent behavior. Don Ranard implicitly suggests a different test: How far has a government fallen short of realizing its society's potential for political democracy? Marvin Zonis seems to follow a third course. For him the issue is not whether the Shah's government violated human rights more than most other states, but simply whether there was serious deprivation of fundamental rights. So, among them, the studies develop the various criteria the United States and other governments might adopt in determining where to apply leverage.

The cases also highlight the very limited means deployed by the Carter administration on behalf of humanitarian goals. Despite some tough rhetoric of a general character, in practice "quiet diplomacy" was the means overwhelming prefered. Neither these nor any other cases can tell us much about the potential efficacy of serious economic sanctions. For as someone remarked of Christianity (having in mind the Sermon on the Mount), we have no basis to judge its practical consequences since it has never been tried. Despite his soft-stepping, as well as his inconsistencies, President Carter succeeded, according to these authors, in conveying an intimidating sense of new purpose in American policy. But Ranard and Zonis feel that a tougher line might well have had a powerful and ultimately constructive influence on Korean and Iranian Policy.

In conclusion, it seems to me that these cases give bone and flesh to the Carter rhetoric. The body is still skeletal. But it most definitely moves.

Tom J. Farer

1. "The Hell of Good Intentions," *Foreign Policy* 3 (Winter 1977-1978) pp. 7-8.

Toward a Humanitarian Diplomacy: a Primer for Policy

TOM J. FARER

INTRODUCTION

The confusion which infects every discussion of the proper role of human rights in the conduct of American foreign policy reminds me of a school exam in which not only the answers but the questions as well are unknown. There is not even an agreed-upon definition of the concept of human rights. Some construe it narrowly. To them the human-rights issue is simply a question of when and how the united States should attempt to prevent other governments from torturing and murdering their citizens. It is, in other words, one more goal of foreign policy, one on a long list that includes halting nuclear proliferation, assuring Western access to the raw materials of the third world, and maintaining the strategic balance. To others, it is a value base for appraising every aspect of the foreign policy of the United States. Whether we are negotiating a new chapter of détente with the Soviet Union, managing the political transformation of southern Africa, organizing the division of ocean resources, pressuring third-world countries to limit their exports to our domestic market or encouraging multinational corporations based in the United States to increase their foreign holdings, we are influencing the capacity of human beings to maintain or

1

acquire "rights," rights enumerated in the various international covenants, conventions, and declarations which make up the tangible body of international humanitarian law.

Those rights are economic as well as political. They include the right to employment and food as well as to the exercise of free speech. The size of our economy, the sophistication of our technology, the ubiquity of our investors, as well as the power of our arsenal, make us so globally consequential that the acts and omissions of the United States government and private interests subject to its influence must constantly affect the opportunities of peoples throughout the world to defend and increase their rights.

From a moral perspective, it is irrelevant whether effects are intended or merely incidental to the achievement of other ends. Prevailing moral convictions impose responsibility for the foreseeable consequences of our acts. They do not exculpate the nobly motivated terrorist who destroys an airliner crammed with innocent bystanders in order to execute a vicious dictator who happens to be aboard. From the same perspective, the United States could not exculpate itself if, through acts designed solely to secure compensation for expropriated investments, it knowingly facilitated a bloody coup d'etat, as many believe was the case in Chile.

Human rights will be trivialized if they are relegated to some bureaucratic ghetto, a little department of humanitarian concern within the great decision factory. But while moral coherence requires that all foreign-policy decisions consider the consequences of different options for human rights, the commitment to seek the enhancement of human rights as an *affirmative goal*— rather than solely as a byproduct of other policies—does entail the construction of a distinct policy framework. At the beginning of the Carter administration, I wrote that it must decide in what cases and under what circumstances this should be an affirmative goal, what means can be developed for its achievement, and what risks should the United States be willing to assume. Until it develops some very specific, morally coherent, and mutually consistent answers to these questions, I continued, the Administration is doomed to blunder from case to case, dissipating public support, confusing potential targets, and leaving the bureaucracy largely free to compromise policy in the name of bureaucratic accommodation. For once, I would prefer not to have been prescient.

POLICY DILEMMAS

We cannot decide when we ought to do something about human rights until we are clearer about what it is we hope to accomplish. Even if all the possible objectives in the realm of human rights were compatible, we would still have to develop some sense of priorities. In diplomacy, no less than business, limited resources impose choice.

In setting out affirmatively to promote human rights, the United States can choose among at least three distinct objectives. One is increased protection of the individual from torture and other forms of cruel and degrading treatment, and from arbitrary arrest; we could, that is, concentrate on defending people against violations of their physical integrity. A second is increased civil and political rights: the right to vote, to express and publish views on public issues, to associate with others for political and economic ends, and so on. We would be nudging states towards more plural societies and more representative governments. A third possible objective is to expand economic and cultural rights, rights to adequate food, shelter, health care, and education. Here the emphasis is on placing a floor under poverty and increasing economic opportunity.

In the most careful public formulation of its position, Secretary Vance's 1977 Law Day address at the University of Georgia, the administration embraced all three ends without discrimination. This is easy enough to manage in words. Deeds are another thing.

To demonstrate his commitment to human rights, President Carter has said that a country's respect for human rights or the lack thereof will affect the character of its bilateral relations with the United States. Let us imagine two states, A and B. Country A is characterized by periodic elections, a fairly free press, multiple parties, and a market economy. Unfortunately, it is also a country suffering from vast discrepancies of wealth, widespread illiteracy, hunger, disease, and high infant mortality rates for at least 60 percent of the population. In these respects, there has been little change over the past 15 years. Fifteen years ago, country B had roughly the same economic and social characteristics. Then there was a revolution. By now it has solved the basic problems of underdevelopment: There is universal literacy and practically everyone has a sufficient diet, shelter, and access to basic medical services, so that disease and mortality statistics are not appreciably worse than those in developed countries.

This great change has been accomplished by the revolutionary government. That government tolerates only one political party; it controls all media of communication and prohibits the dissemination of information and ideas which it deems pernicious; schools, trade unions and virtually all cultural associations are run by the state.

In the process of achieving revolutionary change, the government alienated and dispossessed much of the middle and upper classes. Hundreds of thousands went into exile. Others conspired against the government and were imprisoned.

It is not hard to find real cases to substitute for these hypotheticals. While no doubt distinguishable in many details, Colombia and Cuba will do. China and India also exemplify the essential contrast. But in order to clarify the choices at stake, it is more useful to deal with the hypotheticals and to assume that both are strategically inconsequential and equally prepared to enjoy good relations with the United States. On those assumptions the human rights issue emerges from the usual controlling rationale for the policy of the United States.

What should that policy be? If our only end is to encourage more plural and politically democratic societies, we will probably ignore the achievements of the revolutionary government and refuse to contemplate improved relations. At best we will do nothing to assist it, reserving potential economic aid or other benefits as incentives for progress towards if not democratization at least more openness, for instance, by allowing the sale of foreign magazines and newspapers or easing travel restrictions both on its own citizens and visitors. Conversely, in dispensing economic, political, and military support, we will favor Country *A*.

The administration has rightly rejected a human-rights policy which categorically subordinates eating to speaking. In its arrogant provincialism, such a policy would be self-defeating. Third world governments of every political hue identify economic and social progress as their immediate and primary obligation. Whatever they may do in fact, however ruthlessly they may bleed their compatriots, accumulating wealth atop a dungheap of misery, these governments seek legitimacy in their claimed commitment to the alleviation of that misery. Governments both good and bad must consequently scorn a human-rights policy directed only at the exercise of rights they deem subordinate.

We need not and should not acknowledge that subordination as a general principle, even if there are occasional cases where a country must burst through the mere forms of liberal democracy in order to establish economic and social rights for the great bulk of the population. Those cases are exceptional if for no other reason than the infrequent appearance among developing countries of even formal democracy.

In their constitutions and often in international forums, the governments of developing countries profess respect for civil and political freedoms, suggesting only that they must flower in the wake of economic progress. We do not risk international isolation by espousing the political and civil rights traditionally preferred by liberal capitalist states, as long as we in our turn do not dismiss economic and social rights. We should urge that they progress together, even if unevenly, on parallel tracks as they generally have done in the West. But if we pursue only the former, our effort will be construed as a mere rationalization to reduce support for the aspirations of the third world, and we will thus have to proceed without the support of international moral suasion. Rather than elevating political and civil liberties, we will contaminate them through association with what will be seen as the selfish, parochial interests of the most affluent states.

Policy must be reasonably consistent. The governments we seek to influence must have a fairly accurate idea of the circumstances in which the United States will applaud or censure their behavior. The factors which will lead the United States to reward or punish must not only be clear, they must also seem equitable. This means that like countries must be treated alike. Essays in moral diplomacy which appear to discriminate among states for reasons unrelated to human rights will enrage nationalist sentiment in target countries, strengthening the delinquent leadership and inhibiting a positive response to initiatives made by the United States. The selection of targets will be attributed to hidden interests of an economic or strategic character. And so rather than enlisting the moral authority of the global community's aspirations, our efforts will be poisoned by cynicism.

But how, in practice, can we achieve reasonable clarity and consistency while trying simultaneously to foster political, civil, economic, and social rights, as well as the right to personal security?* The obstacles are formidable. There is, first of all, the problem of comparability between achievement in one realm of human rights and failure in another (our Cuban and Colombian case) and comparability between different forms and degrees of achievement in any single realm.

A case like India makes us doubt the facile equation of affluence with the capacity to sustain democracy. Nevertheless, for all the reasons endlessly elaborated by political theorists, representative political institutions do not often coexist with mass poverty and illiteracy. The linkage is less tight than many in the West have conventionally believed, but linkage there still is. Cultural homogeneity, power relationships among ethnic groups, and cultural traditions also influence the democratic potential of any given society.

* To moderate repetition, I will hereafter refer simply to political and economic rights.

Perceived differences in potential are already implicit in the selection of targets for humanitarian concern. The worldwide outcry over the coup in Chile was fueled not only by its bloodiness but also by Chile's long tradition of democratic government. President Pinochet has claimed that Chile is the victim of a double standard. But in large measure the standard to which it is held is the standard Chile forged for itself over the years, the standard of a free society. If we judge countries by their potential, we will sometimes celebrate small steps towards freedom in one, while disparaging the same measures in another. The target state and its supporters will charge discrimination. But if we ignore real and widely felt differences, we must lose credibility while failing to press for the highest attainable goals.

Problems of comparability arise in the economic and social realms as well. Take two countries at roughly comparable stages of development. In both, the masses are desperately impoverished. One country chooses a strategy of rapid growth relying heavily on profit incentives and production for export. While the G.N.P. begins to grow rapidly, wealth becomes more concentrated, and prices rise including the price of food, the best agricultural land being reserved for export-oriented crops. A decade after the take-off, the welfare of the bottom 40 percent of the population has deteriorated, and the next 20 percent has just managed to hold its own. When criticized, the leadership of this country responds in the very words used by a former President of Brazil: "First the pie must grow; then we will divide it."

The other country equates development with improved welfare for the masses. Through price controls and increased taxes on the middle and upper classes, it provides the population with an adequate though simple diet, with primary schooling, and minimally decent shelter and health facilities. Growth is very slow, but as in the case of Cuba (though without recourse to its authoritarian methods), the country soon achieves rates of literacy and health not far below those in affluent countries. (In most essential respects, Sri Lanka, the former Ceylon, fits the description.) This second country has achieved an advanced state of economic rights. But its population is growing faster than its economy. If this disproportion continues, the next generation may sink back into extreme poverty. Other things being equal, does the country that has opted for immediate welfare have a better claim on our friendship?

Certain deficiencies of knowledge are a second impediment to the management of a clear, consistent, and morally appealing policy. There seems to be a sufficient body of validated data about the facts of disease, malnutrition, and mortality to support persuasive comparisons. The World and the various regional banks, the regional economic commissions established under United Nations auspices, the specialized agencies of the United Nations like the World Health and Food and Agricultural Organizations accumulate mountains of data with a cachet enhanced by the political neutrality of these institutions. Third-world countries themselves increasingly have been collecting essential data. The consequences of Brazil's economic growth for the bottom 60 percent of its citizens are, for instance, recorded in the Brazilian government's own statistics.

Data about physical security are harder to come by and are infinitely more controversial. No government admits to the practice of torture, which is often carried out in hidden detention centers. A large number of regimes encourage, where they do not actually employ, clandestine paramilitary groups to perpetrate embarrassing atrocities. Governments also conceal detention, torture, and execution by means of arrests carried out by unidentified security officers employing unmarked cars, often operating after dark. As far as the government is concerned, the individual has simply "disappeared."

Through its covert intelligence facilities and often through contacts between its military attaches and security officials in the host government, the United States can, if it desires, fairly well estimate the extent of government-sponsored violations of personal security. But the nature of its sources often precludes public authentication. Private international organizations like Amnesty International and the International Commission of Jurists have pieced together a sufficiently accurate picture from the survivors of the charnel houses where political prisoners are "processed" and from witnesses to their arrest. Sometimes these accounts are supplemented by officials unable to stomach their government's behavior. But the danger of reprisal often compels anonymity; and the credibility of those willing to go public is assailed on the grounds of political bias. Since their members are originally selected by the states subject to their jurisdiction, official multinational investigatory bodies like the Inter-American Human Rights Commission provide information with the greatest stamp of authenticity.

Although each source has its limitations, cumulatively they endow the government of the United States with a sufficient factual basis for judgments, at least in the most egregious cases, which it can defend effectively before the courts of domestic and international opinion.

When one attempts to appraise performance in the realm of political and civil rights, the problem of securing adequate information undergoes a qualitative change. Here the *relevance* of available data rather than its *credibility* is the most salient issue. How do we measure freedom of the press? Simply by the number of papers in private hands? Surely not, since those hands may be tied, more or less subtly, by government censors. What, moreover, do we mean by a free press? Is it one whose content is not determined by the government or one that prints all the news and views people living in that society are likely to deem relevant? Only the latter conception relates free press to the ends of representative government. But if we adopt that conception, private ownership may become even less relevant an index, for we can imagine cases where the owners all belong to a tight little elite determined to suppress news and views deemed pernicious to the interests of their class. In such cases, a government newspaper monopoly established by a confident populist regime may allow as wide a range of views as its multiple predecessors.

I readily concede that where newspapers are privately owned, competition for readers, enjoined by financial incentives, normally will produce far greater diversity than a government monopoly. But rich men sometimes buy papers for influence rather than profit. In contrast, where there is a government monopoly, but each important bureaucracy can produce its own paper, bureaucratic rivalry might to some degree substitute for market incentives as a stimulus to diversity. The basic point is this: Wherever the press is monopolized by a narrow interest committed to manipulating the needs and concerns of its audience, in a real sense the press is not free. At least theoretically the substance of freedom can be lost even where the press is in private hands.

Of course there are many easy cases where even the most superficial observor can detect the progressive emasculation of diversity. I raise the issue of free press not to suggest the contrary but rather to help puncture the conservative myth that one will *necessarily* find a higher level of civil and political liberties in countries ruled by right-wing authoritarian regimes, that is, regimes that defend and encourage private enterprise, than in countries ruled by authoritarian socialists. The conservative assumption rests on the belief that a private sector within the economy must represent a center of power and influence and independent opinion outside the reach of the government. In fact, the government may be little more than the militarized arm of the private sector. Or businessmen may be the docile partners of a military caste—Mamlukes who prefer to leave economic activity to carefully monitored civilians made malleable by fear and lusty profit.

Contemporary governments of every ideological hue command ever more effective resources for the domination of society. Deeply disturbed by this development, the late Kalman Silvert wrote:

> The days are numbered of the traditional authoritarianism, in which the dissident can withdraw from politics and remain safe, hidden inaccessibly in many institutional nooks and crannies. Now, even in the Central American republics, the total control governors had over illiterate populations can be extended by modern techniques to individuals, bypassing institutional protections.

The crux of the matter is that the assumption championed by Western conservatives cannot substitute for a careful analysis of each government's performance. Periodic elections are a useful but often precarious index because there are so many ways in which the results can be predetermined. Parliaments and multiple political parties also may turn out to be forms without substance. Taking political and civil rights seriously entails a lot of sophisticated homework.

A final impediment to the realization of a policy consistent with the declared aims of this Administration is the multiplicity of our foreign-policy objectives. America's relentlessly competitive relationship with the Soviet Union regularly produces justifications for subordinating human rights. So does concern about nuclear proliferation. Both, for example, have helped to limit the reaction of the United States to the abuse of human rights in South Korea. Energy and the Russian problem made the United States feel protective about the Shah of Iran whose secret-police force, the Savak, was notoriously vicious. Conversely, the need to keep Soviet-American competition within safe limits and to secure Soviet cooperation in areas where our interests may coincide must affect the calculations about means the United States should use to extract human-rights concessions.

There is no need for the tedious multiplication of examples. Everyone recognizes that as the new boy in the game, human rights must compete with traditional participants for a piece of the decision-making action. Uncertainty exists only about the ground rules. It is now time to consider what they ought to be.

POLICY IMPLEMENTATION: FIRST STEPS

No policy will transcend every impediment, resolve every contradiction. If I had been Jimmy Carter, these are the guidelines and related procedures I would have adopted to shape the decisions of my senior aides and their divers departments and agencies, bureaus and sub-bureaus, that day after day grind out the substance of our foreign relations.

To begin with, I would have declared that gross violations of the individual's right to physical security must *in every case* occasion public condemnation by the United States *and* an effort to terminate that violation by all appropriate means, *unless* the President himself determines either that such action is likely to have a powerful, adverse effect on imperative national security interests or that any affirmative action on our part would tend to aggravate the violation. There would, in other words, be a strong but not irrefutable presumption against inaction. Violations would be deemed gross wherever they are numerous and sustained and particularly where there is external evidence that they resulted from policy decisions at the highest levels of the target government.

No means for alleviating the violations, including a total ban on economic relationships, would be absolutely foreclosed. Even force would be considered as a last resort in cases where there is no plausible alternative means of preventing or terminating large-scale slaughter and the intervention can be managed without substantial risk to the intervening force, the victims themselves, or innocent third parties. Where these basic requirements coincide with authorization of force by the political organs of the United Nations or a regional organization, the presumption against its use would be further weakened.

The United States would reject every alleged justification for institutionalized mayhem. In response to the common claim that terrorism and subversion require "strong action," the United States would follow the line laid down by the Inter-American Human Rights Commission of the OAS and reaffirmed by an absolute majority at the Organization's General Assembly. Governments have an unquestioned right and, indeed, an obligation to maintain public order. In grave cases this may require temporary suspension of certain civil liberties. Many national constitutions provide specifically for such suspension following executive declaration of a state of siege or emergency. But these constitutional provisions never leave the executive power completely unrestrained. Neither does international law. The American Declaration on the Rights and Duties of Man, unanimously adopted by the members of the OAS in 1949, categorically precludes suspension of those guarantees relating to the security of the person. Other international declarations and agreements reach the same result. Terrorism is equally intolerable whether practiced by officials or private entrepreneurs.

The priority I would accord to personal security seems inevitable. First, it is backed by the force of international law. Second, it reflects the will of Congress as manifested, for example, in Section 116 of the International Development and Food Assistance Act of 1975:

No assistance may be provided under this part to the government of any country which engages in a consistent pattern of gross violations of internationally recognized human rights, including torture or cruel, inhuman, or degrading treatment or punishment, prolonged detention without charges, or other flagrant denial of the right to life, liberty, and the security of person, unless such assistance will directly benefit the needy people in such country.

Third, it calls for action by the United States in precisely the kind of case that tends to arouse ordinary Americans right across the political spectrum. Fourth, since these violations usually are notorious and are universally condemned, at least in the abstract, any action by the United States is far less likely to be arraigned for improper "intervention" in the internal affairs of other states than would be true where it acts to defend political or economic rights. Fifth, the objective sought, if it is to be obtained at all, will have to be obtained quickly, at least where life is at stake. Thus, public attention will be concentrated on the drama, holding at bay the special interests—for example, United States investors in the target country—that over time are capable of eroding policies which enjoy broad but diffuse support. Finally, because gross violations of personal security are, by their nature, difficult to conceal and, under the policy, indefensible, there is a greater possibility of *preventing* violations—which is both better and normally easier than terminating them. Governments contemplating the use of terror will be driven to weigh the potential dangers of opposition from the United States.

It is with reluctance and trepidation that I admit the remote possibility of recourse to force without authorization from the United Nations. In the past, as in the disgraceful Dominican intervention, references to human rights have been a mere fig leaf intended to conceal crasser ends. But the leaf's transparency in cases of abuse make it seem rather inconsequential as an influence on national action. What danger there is seems finally outweighed by the number of cases where force and only force can alleviate unspeakable slaughter. One recalls, for instance, Burundi, that remote little African country where during the spring and summer of 1972, the government organized the methodical slaughter of some quarter of a million Hutus. If we can applaud the forceful rescue of less than 200 people at Entebee, can we exclude the use of force where tens of thousands are otherwise doomed? Like other Western governments, the United States has never conceded the demise of the nineteenth-century doctrine of "humanitarian intervention" in defense of one's own nationals.

Admittedly, most Third-World governments deny the doctrine's continued validity. A group of Western legal scholars also question its compatibility with prevailing norms governing the use of force. In their judgment (supported by the 1949 opinion of the International Court of Justice in the *Corfu Channel Case*), since the adoption of the United Nations Charter, military measures are valid only for defense against armed attack on the territory of a state or its armed forces. So-called "precedents" like the 1964 rescue of hostages held by rebels in the Congo and the more recent Shaba rescue mission carried out by French troops are easily distinguished as interventions *authorized by a recognized government*. The fact that the alleged legal change, eliminating humanitarian intervention as a legitimate means of protecting national interests, has not been accepted by a significant number of states and the muted reaction of non-Western governments to the Entebbe affair leave room for doubt about the current state of the law in cases where a government threatens a large number of aliens with summary execution or other gross violations of fundamental human rights.

The categorical imperative of the human-rights movement is the equal value of all human lives. Means we are willing to employ to defend our own citizens, or whites, regardless of citizenship, ought not be absolutely ruled out when other lives are at stake.

ECONOMIC RIGHTS: A BASIS FOR ACTION

Secretary Vance's declaration that the Carter administration would defend and promote not only the individual's right to personal security and his associational and political rights, but also the full-range of economic and social rights has provoked skeptism and even some outright hostility.

One theme of the skeptics is summarized in the remark of a distinguished English development economist who thought that Secretary Vance's statement exemplified the naïve optimism of a people determined to believe that all good things must go together. In fact, he and others have argued, the unqualified assertion of political and civil rights probably would often conflict with progress toward fuller realization of economic and social rights. In addition, they have contended, treating the economic and social goals enumerated in the Universal Declaration of Human Rights and the Covenant on Economic and Social Rights as "rights" would threaten the morally compelling goal of eliminating pauperism.

Outright hostility marked the pronouncements of certain, principally third-world, commentators who were not inclined to assume a benevolent purpose behind the Administration's formulation. On the contrary, they saw its equally proportioned emphasis on political-civil and economic-social rights as a threat to their campaign for a new international economic order. It was a diversion, they insisted, designed to conceal the obdurate refusal of the developed countries to reform the existing exploitative system and to alter the moral balance which in actual fact tilts so heavily in favor of Southern demands.

The administration has done little to offset either skeptics or antagonists other than blandly to reaffirm its sincerity and the assumed compatibility of all kinds of human rights. It has not bothered to counter its critics with explicit theories of its own. It has not answered implicitly by outlining a plan of coordinated action on behalf of these supposedly equally important rights.

And the multiple acts and omissions of its everyday statecraft are so isolated, episodic, and ambiguous that they seem no less compatible with the disbelief of skeptics than with the administration's up-beat affirmations.

On occasion, to be sure, the administration has applied its economic and political influence in an attempt to alleviate gross violations of personal rights or even, in certain instances, other political and civil rights. Faced with institutionalized torture, summary executions, or brutal suppression of trade unions and peaceful political movements, it has reduced bilateral aid, blocked or slowed loan applications to international financial institutions, or taken other modest steps. But, as far as can be learned, it has never attempted to sanction economic programs calculated to maintain or even to aggravate mass misery. Does this reticence in speech and action reflect disinterest in or dispair about the possibility of promoting economic and social rights? Or does it stem from the conviction that in states where the political process is relatively open and individuals are not ruled by fear of torture and violent death, humane economic development will more or less automatically occur?

Reticence should not be a function either of uncertainty about the essential legal content of claims to economic and social rights or of inadequate information about the operation of contemporary political and economic systems. As far as content is concerned, it is true that the universal declaration lists without discrimination both economic rights to the goods required for survival and rights to goods, such as cradle-to-grave social security and technical and professional education, which far exceed the present productive capacity of many poor countries, however conscientious their governments. This lack of discrimination has led some to argue that all economic and social "rights" are not true rights in the sense of categorical present claims on governments. They are, rather, mere aspirational values.

Adherents of this position fail to grasp the essential nature of the legal obligation assumed by all governments: the obligation to work in good faith for the realization of these aspirations in a sequence which gives priority to basic health and nutrition. The priority of "survival rights" or "basic needs" is a virtual corollary of the right to personal security. There is neither a moral nor practical difference between a government executing innocent people or one which tolerates their death by starvation when it has or has the means to obtain the food that could save them. Widespread condemnation of Haile Selassie's government for its conscious failure to publicize the terrible famine of 1973 and 1974 and thus obtain needed relief supplies evidences the broad consensus about a government's legal and moral obligations.

Yet, a few commentators still insist the cases are different. In refraining from executing opponents, the dissenters argue, the government is not compelled to choose between various possible resource allocations. There is no economic decision, for the decision in this case is "cost free." By contrast, an emergency nutrition or public health program may require the diversion of resources from other desirable ends such as feeder roads or new credit facilities for cash-crop farmers. Such allocational decisions, the argument concludes, are properly outside the realm of human rights; they are appropriately at the discretion of individual governments.

The supposed distinction does not correspond to the perceptions of governments, much less to the moral imperatives of mankind. Execution, torture, detention without trial, and other violations of individual rights are techniques deemed necessary or at least very efficient by many governments for achieving political, social, and economic ends. To forego torture, they plainly believe, is to incur costly inefficiency—for instance, in achieving national pacification—with consequences accountable materially as well as morally.

Another suggested difference between "true rights," such as claims against the government for personal security, and mere aspirational welfare values is that violations of the former stem directly from governmental action, while welfare claims arise as a consequence of acts of God (for example, drought) or the impersonal international market. The distinction is neither accurate nor relevant. It is inaccurate because governments can violate rights of physical security by negligently or maliciously failing to act against private persons bent on murdering their fellow citizens. The government in such cases is not directly responsible for the infliction of unjustified pain. It, nevertheless, is legally and morally delinquent. Aside from failing to express logical differences, what is morally or legally interesting about the supposed distinction? Governments are endowed with the right, the resources, and the obligation to protect their subjects. Their legitimacy is rooted in that very function. Governments that simply refrain from crippling their populations are mere parasites without any secular basis for their claimed authority.

While the essential nature of the obligations assumed by governments is reasonably clear, are there means available for measuring performance? Moreover, except in egregious cases of mass starvation, can governments defend relatively low levels of achievement on grounds of the need to accelerate growth in order to lay a foundation for very much greater achievement a generation hence? Finally, is there a case for the proposition that full realization of political and civil rights in developing countries often inhibits economic progress and thus in practice conflicts with efforts to progress in the economic and social realm?

Two decades of research conducted by scholars, governments, and international institutions have produced a body of data on which to rest operationally specific answers to these questions. We summarize them in the following set of propositions: *Yes,* we can both measure and to a functionally useful degree explain progress and failure in realizing economic and social rights for living generations. *No,* progress is not inversely related to growth rates or to the realized level of political and civil rights; it does, however, correlate very significantly with consciously egalitarian public policy.

Development experts generally agree that life expectancy, infant mortality, and literacy are the most appropriate indicators for measuring the physical well-being of any country's population and for the measurement of progress towards higher levels of economic and social well-being for the general population. To begin with, the data, although uneven in quality, are generally available. In addition, as James Grant, recently elected director of UNICEF, has noted:

> Life expectancy and infant mortality can be very good indicators of important aspects of social progress in that they represent the sum of the effects of nutrition, public health, income, and the general environment. At the same time, the two indicators reflect quite different aspects of social interaction; preliminary work suggests, for example, that infant mortality rather sensitively characterizes the availability of clean water, the condition of the home

environment, and the well-being of mothers, while life expectancy at age one is a reflection of nutrition and of general environmental characteristics outside the home. Literacy is both a measure of well-being and a skill that is important in the development process; how widespread literacy is also provides a good indication of the position of women in the society. The extent to which poor groups are literate helps determine the extent to which they do share, or will be able to share, the benefits of economic growth.[1]

For the past several years the Overseas Development Council and other organizations have, in fact, measured national achievements in each indicated area, and have consolidated them in a single Physical Quality of Life Index (PQLI). In addition, they have measured rates of progress in reducing absolute poverty by the expression in percentage terms of the annual reduction in the disparity that exists between current national performance in PQLI categories and the performance levels already attained, or likely to be attained before the end of this century, by the most advanced countries (Disparity Reduction Rates). The results are devasting for the proposition that national wealth equates roughly with human welfare.[2]

The country of Sri Lanka, for instance, had an average per capita G.N.P. of $179 for the period between 1970 and 1975. But its average PQLI during that period was 82, reflecting a life expectancy at birth of 68, an infant mortality rate of 47 per 1000 and 81 percent literacy in its population of 14 million. Iran, by comparison, had a per capita G.N.P. of 1260, roughly seven times Sri Lanka's. Yet the content and distribution of that wealth produced a PQLI 30 percent lower than Sri

Lanka's. Life expectancy for the average Iranian bene-
ficiary of the Shah's "White Revolution" was in the range
of 51 to 57. Infant mortality per 1000 births ran some-
where between 100 and 120. And the country experienced a literacy rate between 40 and 50 percent.

Countries in the same region with roughly comparable cultural and climatic endowments also show
marked differences. Consider, for example, Mexico and
Cuba. The former had an average per capita G.N.P. of
$996 for the period between 1970 and 1975. Life expec-
tancy averaged 65 years, infant mortality 66 deaths per
1000 live births and literacy was estimated at 74 percent.
The resulting PQLI was 75. On the per capita income
scale, Cuba ranked significantly lower, somewhat under
$800. But Cubans enjoyed a 70-year life expectancy,
infant mortality rate of 27 per 1000 live births and 78
percent literacy: Hence a PQLI of 85.

In certain respects, the PQLI not among them, Mexico more closely resembles Taiwan. Both now emphasize
export-oriented growth. And both have markets and
private property as the principal parameters of their
respective socioeconomic systems. Taiwan has been
growing faster. But between 1970 and 1975 its per capita income of $847 stood substantially below Mexico's
figure of $996. Its PQLI, in contrast, was 12 points
higher because it had raised life expectancy to 70, raised
literacy levels to 85 percent and reduced infant mortality
to 25 per 1000 births.

James Grant is certainly right when, in his proposal
for measuring and targeting progress in meeting basic
needs, he writes:

Much more research is required before there can
be even a basic consensus about the principal
variables—and their relative importance in specific

circumstances—that have made possible rapid progress in improving social conditions in such geographically, politically, and culturally diverse countries and regions as China, Taiwan, Sri Lanka, Kerala, Cuba, Barbados, Jamaica, and Costa Rica— and recently the city of Newark. Similarly, Iran, Algeria, Nigeria—and Washington, D.C.—all warrant examination to identify the reasons for the slowness of their PQLI progress.[3]

But he nevertheless is able to conclude that all of the lower-income countries, from Sri Lanka to Cuba, that have achieved relative success to date in meeting basic needs despite a relatively low level of output share a unique common feature: All have given "priority attention to their poor majorities."[4]

Such attention quickly yields dramatic results, as illustrated by the case of Sri Lanka. The government instituted a program of Malaria control, greatly expanded grassroots public health care, and subsidized a grain ration for the very poor in the two decades after achieving independence in 1947. As a result, it reduced infant mortality from an average of approximately 180 deaths per thousand live births to 60 per thousand.

Dramatic improvement in overcoming extreme poverty has been achieved in radically different political, economic, and cultural climates. Romania reduced infant mortality from 54 in the late 1940s to 13 in the late 1960s. In the United States, belated attention to the problems of American indians reduced infant mortality from the outrageous figure of 63 per 1000 in 1954 to about 18 per 1000 in 1975.

Countries like Sri Lanka, with very low per capita income and low growth rates, probably require very highly focused programs. The life-giving goods and services must be delivered directly to the poor with maximum economy. Wealthier and high-growth economies can rely more on market mechanisms if they achieve real full employment, that is, a condition where the entire adult population is renumerated at levels which permit them to meet their basic subsistance needs.

Rapid growth alone will not accomplish marked reductions in mass misery. For the past three decades and particularly in the period between 1968 and 1973, Brazil experienced one of the fastest rates of industrial growth in the entire world and thus succeeded in driving its per capita income over $1000. But it starved social welfare programs, restrained wages, and shunned land reform. While experts differ as to whether the lowest 40 percent of the population of Brazil experienced an absolute decline in its already miserable living standards, no one, including the highest officials of the Brazilian government, claimed that their position was much improved. As one would therefore expect, Brazil's PQLI has remained low, a mere 66 compared with 75 in Thailand, 82 in the Republic of Korea, 73 in Malasia, 82 in Sri Lanka and 84 in Cuba, all countries with markedly lower per capita income.

One difference between the conditions of growth in Taiwan and South Korea, (as well as Japan) and those in Brazil is related to the extent of land reform. All three of the Asian countries adopted very comprehensive land-reform programs at the very time they began their explosive growth. In all three the rural sector is now characterized by modest-sized, highly productive family farms whose owners enjoy reasonable access to markets and credit and experience consistently rising personal income. Productivity is combined with land-people ratios much higher than those found in northern Mexico's large-scale, high-technology agriculture. The former sustains high productivity and yet decently supports 70 to 80 workers per 100 cultivated acres, while the latter uses only three or four workers to cultivate the same area. These countries have chosen different strategies of development with different consequences for their respective populations.

What specific propositions relevant to the promotion of human rights emerge from these comparisons? I would list the following, including several already mentioned.

First: Economic growth and rapid amelioration of mass poverty are not incompatable. On the contrary, in a significant number of cases they have coincided. And in the view of many experts, improved health, nutrition, and literacy, and the greater overall equality of income and wealth they reflect, powerfully contributed to accelerated growth. If the pie is distributed as it grows, it may grow faster.

Second: Neither relative national affluence nor high growth rates are a prerequisite for the radical reduction of mass misery. Success does require political commitment, precise targeting, and bureaucratic efficiency.

Third: No single system of political economy, no single development model, has demonstrated a unique or even a plainly superior capacity to promote economic and social rights. Success stories include the rambunctious capitalism of Korea and Taiwan, capitalism softened by democratic socialist government in Sri Lanka, and Cuba's authoritarian socialism. In other words, success has been achieved both in market and nonmarket conditions and under governments varying in ideology across most of the political spectrum from right to far left.

Fourth: Success in market economies ruled by conservative authoritarian governments apparently requires, as a precedent, a marked redistribution of productive assets, particularly land, as well as very high growth rates. This latter condition may not be achievable in the current and prospective international economy, marked as it is by slower growth and protectionist pressure in the developed countries that have been prime markets for the fast-growth states.

Fifth: In terms of meeting basic human needs, authoritarian socialist techniques have produced impressive results in countries with well-established bureaucratic structures, a broadly shared national feeling, and a sizeable educated elite. Their successful application in the new African states is highly problematical. Tanzania is the only one which has tried; the results are not yet promising.

Sixth: Globally, there is no clear correlation between, on the one hand, growth rates and success in meeting human needs and, on the other, political and civil rights. Democracies (such as Sri Lanka, Costa Rica, and Trinidad and Tobago), left- and rightwing authoritarian regimes (such as Cuba and Taiwan, respectively) have in their different ways succeeded in raising the PQLI to impressive heights over relatively short periods of time. One would assume, a priori, that authentically democratic regimes in third-world countries would uniformly emphasize programs to meet basic needs and would therefore be more likely to have a high PQLI. We have only a few examples. With the notable exception of India, they tend to confirm the assumption. India's Disparity Reduction Rate is decidedly on the low side among developing countries. Is this attributable to indifference at the top or incompetent administration? Most observers would emphasize both the caution of the elite about enforcing nominally redistributive programs and an unwieldy, inefficient bureaucracy very subject to influence by local power holders.

One would also hypothesize an initially high measure of achievement for leftwing authoritarian regimes because they are ideologically committed to limiting poverty, because their assumption of power is coincident with a smashing of the old class structure, and because, other things being equal, the centralization of power over the economy facilitates the rapid concentration of resources needed to reduce poverty. The results of the efforts of the Chinese, Cuban, and North Korean governments appear to support this second hypothesis, although data on China and North Korea is incomplete and the extent of the success may be less than is generally believed. Of course, the nature of these regimes means that achievement in the field of economic and social rights accompanies a sustained and pervasive violation of civil and political rights.

As democratic regimes always and authoritarian socialist regimes in the immediate post-revolutionary period have a built-in tendency to alleviate mass deprivation, conservative authoritarian regimes have a built-in animus against the poorer classes because, by definition, they spring from and seek to conserve existing hierarchies. In Latin America and in those African states where the regimes accurately reflect well-established economic and social hierarchies, Disparity Reduction Rates are, as one would expect, low to middling, although there are important differences among countries rather similarly situated in terms of natural endowments. As indicated above, in Asia the record is considerably more mixed. Low per capita income countries like Pakistan and Indonesia compare very unfavorably with populous Sri Lanka. But the middle-income countries of South Korea and Taiwan hold their own in PQLI and Disparity Reduction Rates when compared either to the successful democracies or to China, North Korea,

and Cuba. In both countries high growth rates and com-
mendable PQLI's coincide with rigid authoritarian governments. Both countries allow, albeit within unpredictable limits, some restrained criticism of specific policies;
but the right to criticize is not clearly better institutionalized or broader than in a communist country like the
Soviet Union. Also like their communist counterparts,
both regimes seem well entrenched and durable. The
regime in Taiwan has held power more or less effort-
lessly for some three decades. Commentators do note in
Taiwan's case a gradual relaxation of restraint and some
opening up of the political process. In Korea, however,
the regime seems even more harsh in the mid-seventies
than in the mid-sixties. Success has not mellowed it.

How does one explain the economic welfare record
of these undemocratic conservative regimes? What in-
duced them to initiate the necessary reforms? Possibly,
as some argue, the very immediate external threat often
invoked to justify political repression also drove them to
pacify the population with enhanced welfare. High
literacy and adequate nutrition have the further consequence of contributing to the quality of human resources needed for industrialization and the armed
forces.

Vulnerability to an external threat also encouraged
Taiwan to undertake land reform, which meant break-
ing up the large holdings of a native Taiwanese elite
(who had little influence on the mainlanders who occupied the island in 1949). Very large amounts of aid
from the United States, and expenditures associated
with United States troop deployments on the island
helped build infrastructure and created employment
opportunities in both countries. And then there are the
cultural imponderables: All of the Asian countries, com-
bining high growth rates with high Disparity Reduction

Rates, are in the Chinese cultural zone. Finally, the relatively small size of these countries and relatively homogeneous populations may be factors no less influential
than their proximity to and economic interdependence
with that throbbing engine of growth: Japan.

Conclusions

In light of our knowledge and experience to date,
what measures could the United States adopt, either
alone or in conjunction with other industrially advanced
democracies, to reflect an evenhanded commitment to
economic and social, as well as political and civil rights?
Here are a range of alternatives:

1. Tariff preferences for third-world products could
be enhanced, but limited to countries that effectively
guarantee free speech and free association for nonviolent purposes and demonstrate a commitment to rapid
improvement of their PQLI. The president could be
authorized periodically to revise the list of eligible countries.

The present Generalized System of Preferences is not
required by any international obligation of the United
States. And it is not general, Congress having already
excluded members of OPEC from participation. At the
moment it is an essentially gratuitous, basically un-
guided instrument of policy. As President Carter has
said, "To govern is to choose." If human rights is a
genuine United States objective, then why should it not
guide the allocation of trade benefits in excess of those
available reciprocally and globally under the most-
favored-nation principle of the General Agreement on
Tariffs and Trade. Regimes which use terror to depress
working-class income violate both human rights *and* the

rules of liberal economics, which require that the market determine the price of labor, as well as other factors of production.

2. The United States could commit itself to provide no less than one-third of a 12 to 15 billion dollars a year incremental fund for meeting basic needs in developing countries. This increase in external aid would be feasible if the developed countries as a group approached aid levels equivalent to 0.5 percent of G.N.P. by 1981 (well below the 0.7 urged by third-world spokesmen). The fund would be administered by the contributors and would be dispersed exclusively to countries that agreed to adopt a comprehensive plan for raising their PQLI and that are not engaged in gross violations of political and civil rights.

3. The United States could propose to the Board of Governors of the International Monetary Fund that drawing and stand-by rights in excess of the gold *tranche* (the 25 percent of a country's quota which it contributes to the Fund in gold) be denied any country found by any official human rights fact-finding body with appropriate jurisdiction or by a special fact-finding body established for this purpose by the Board of Governors to be engaged in gross violation of civil and political rights. Drawing rights in excess of the gold *tranche* might also be denied in cases where the potential drawer's proposed reductions in public expenditure are calculated to aggravate malnutrition, disease, or homelessness and the government has feasible alternatives for rehabilitating the balance of payments.

Drawings up to the limit of a country's gold *tranche* give the drawing government little more than it could have obtained on the open market had it retained the gold in its own treasury. Beyond the gold *tranche*, a drawing is simply a loan on concessional terms. Such loans should not be made to any country engaged in any blatant violation of international law such as aggression against a neighboring state or terror practiced against its own people. To make a loan under those circumstances might facilitate the violation.

This arguably would not require a formal amendment of the IMF's Articles of Agreement. Every international agreement, like every domestic contract, is adopted against a background of imperative public policy which it implicitly incorporates. A formal agreement by two or more states to commit, facilitate, or attempt to legitimate aggression is void. Similarly void is an agreement to facilitate or attempt to legitimate gross violations of human rights. To assure the validity of international agreements, they must be interpreted in ways which align them with codified public policy.

Requiring plans to improve balance-of-payments, which do not threaten basic needs, has a second justification, one more closely linked to the institutional purposes of the IMF. The fund is, after all, part of a complex of institutions designed to promote global economic expansion. All of them function in the context of developmental, as well as humanitarian, norms that have over the past two decades acquired the force of law. In actual practice, IMF officials help shape and in many cases decisively determine the content of government plans for reducing payments deficits. Among other things they almost invariably suggest reduction in government expenditures and almost invariably they favor reduction in social welfare expenditures such as food subsidies.

Decreasing government spending for social welfare aggravates malnutrition, reduces the quality of public health, or increases joblessness, with all its attendant pathologies. This of course, has a negative impact, often profound, if not on short-term then surely on intermediate- and long-term productivity. It is a blow to development. Yet, while demanding decreased spending for social welfare, IMF officials often ignore wholly unproductive expenditures on the police and armed forces, as if they were sacrosanct. Thus the Fund undermines the developmental objectives to which it is institutionally committed.

If the IMF Board of Governors rejected the proposal, the United States could then refuse to support or to participate in any expansion of IMF lending capacity and could, on a case-by-case basis, mobilize opposition to drawings which violate the proposed guidelines.

4. The United States could follow essentially the same strategy in connection with the World Bank Group and the regional banks. It could ask the Board of Governors to adopt guidelines prohibiting loans to gross violators of political and civil rights and to governments which refuse to commit themselves to comprehensive plans for meeting basic human needs. Once again, no Charter change is required. Development, the *raison d'être* of these institutions, is not a static concept. Twenty years ago it was defined exclusively in terms of gross national product, in part because more particular indications were not widely available, in part on the assumption that growth would itself mitigate mass poverty. Today we possess more discriminating measures and find no basis for the blithe assumption. Development has always been justified and ultimately even been defined in humanitarian terms. Growth has been a proxy. Now that we have the means to see the thing itself, to satisfy their mandates the banks must adopt new guidelines.

If they are determined to adhere to outmoded formulas, then the United States and like-minded countries could build a new institution which will take the welfare of human beings as the measure of its achievements.

These proposals concerning the international financial institutions do not bootleg political criteria into economic or developmental decision making. Human rights are not "political"; they are *legal*, recognized norms of behavior binding on all governments and international institutions. As long as they are applied objectively and consistently, the complaint of political intervention has no standing.

THE RISKS OF AN ACTIVE POLICY

In terms of our international relationships I see at least three of a general character. One is that of reduced international cooperation in confronting the great transnational problems such as nuclear proliferation, pollution, the allocation of sea and seabed resources, and reconstruction of the monetary and trade-regulating systems. Given the existing congestion of obstacles to effective cooperation, one can doubt whether the aggravations that could possibly be engendered by the active promotion of human rights would add appreciably more to the queue. The issues themselves are so complex, progress so relative, and breakthroughs so dependent on unpredictable catalytic events that it is difficult to form any kind of judgment about the extent of this risk. Still, one reason for discounting it is that these issues can and rationally should be decoupled from the question of human rights. This is least true in the case of nuclear proliferation, where pressure on human-rights issues could encourage third-world states to reach for what they may see as the markedly enhanced prestige and insulation from external influence achieved by the holders of nuclear power. But when it comes to questions of jurisdiction over the seas or pollution, precedent suggests that states vote their interests, allowing little sway to sentiment, ideology or pique.

We are, however, talking about matters of degree. If elites under pressure always reacted rationally, history would record fewer revolutions. So we cannot altogether discount this risk.

Countermeasures could be directed against private commercial interests in the United States. This is a second risk associated with the active promotion of human rights. Given the demand for capital, technology, and knowhow from the United States, these measures will often be self-defeating and hence deterred by that fact alone. There are areas, however, where the deterrent will not suffice, areas where our business is competitive and alternative to that of Europe and Japan. One obvious case is competition for government contracts. If we can attract our fellow democracies to the cause, which we certainly will not have any hope of doing until we ourselves demonstrate a clear and coherent commitment, the risk is thereby moderated. To the extent that effort fails, the United States will often have to keep some of our potential sanctions in reserve, ready to be used to counter discrimination against its business interests. Unfortunately, that is not an entirely sufficient answer. Bias in the letting of government contracts, as in many other official activities that affect the private sector, is far from easy to demonstrate. But the more subtle the bias, the less its utility in deterring pressure from the United States. Nevertheless, it would be unrealistic not to anticipate some losses.

Finally, there is the risk that in some cases withdrawal of support from the United States for rightwing regimes

may facilitate their replacement by regimes of the radical left. In the past, this danger has often been invoked
to justify support for brutal governments. Today, invocation of the Marxist threat seems to carry less political
punch. One reason for this evolution in elite and popular perceptions is the growing appreciation of the opportunities the United States enjoys for correct, businesslike relations with Marxist regimes in the third
world, opportunities springing from the immense
inducements—capital, technology, food, not to mention
sheer tolerance—the United States can deploy on behalf
of its interests. A second and corresponding reason is
the more accurate perception of Soviet limitations in
generating, much less controlling, revolutions. If Marx-
ism is the wave of the future, that future seems to be in
a state of constant recession. And as for those scattered
cases where Marxist movements have triumphed, the
resulting governments seem as little inclined as conservative ones to indulge the preferences of their Great
Power patrons. Ideological unity continues to shatter on
the rock of national self-interest.

The Limits Of Public Support

Although, at least in theory, costs could turn out to be
more than the sum of those entailed by individual cases,
it is the individual cases that are likely to alienate public
opinion, possibly out of all proportion to the costs they
will allegedly dramatize. The human-rights balloon
might quickly deflate, if, for instance, pressure for
democratization in some traditional American ally
helped to produce or at least was seen to coincide with
the emergence of a regime which proceeded to nation-
alize investments from the United States, or which

began to accept technical assistance from communist states, or take other measures hostile to prevalent conceptions of the interests of the United States.[5] There are very few countries where this scenario is plausible, even in the context of an activist human-rights policy. And its plausibility can only decline if the United States sustains its new willingness to treat with leftist regimes on a businesslike basis rather than defining them as inevitable enemies. But, some leftwing skeptics argue, one or two instances might suffice hopelessly to sour public and congressional enthusiasm for a human-rights policy which does not maintain the traditional discrimination in favor of rightwing regimes.

A Marxist would no doubt argue that the problem of sustaining the policy outlined above goes far deeper than the reflexes of dogmatic conservatives. Although it is occasionally overlooked in the raucous drama of domestic political competition, liberals no less than conservatives are committed to the defense and promotion of capitalism. This is inevitable. Every official elite exists in part to promote, legitimate, and ward off attacks which threaten either the national or the international well-being of the dominant economic system.

From this truism leftwing skeptics deduce our incapacity to sustain a comprehensive, nondiscriminatory pressure for the democratization of other states. For in many cases, they argue, democratization will release radical political forces which will challenge that strategy of development which so comfortably fits the third world into the international capitalist system. More representative political systems will require a more equitable distribution of income. This will reduce the demand for luxury consumer goods in the production and marketing of which American and European companies enjoy a competitive advantage. And democratization, with all of its corollaries including a free trade-union movement, will lead to higher wages, lower profits, reduced investment, and less export-oriented growth. These developments will, in turn, adversely affect the existing direct investment from the United States, which was premised on the present high rate of return. It will also adversely affect the countries debt-servicing capabilities, thus jeopardizing billions in private-sector loans.

The limits on humanitarian initiatives cannot, in my judgment, be facilely deduced from the fact that private enterprise is the dominant mode of production in the United States. Conflicts of interest among capitalist enterprises and different economic sectors are one reason why recognizable constraints do not arise out of the vision of the state as servant of the ascendant economic class. The third-world industrial development stimulated by private bank lending, technology licensing, and direct investment from the United States and the other leading capitalist states is hostile to the interests of an important segment of American industry. In alliance with the trade unions it is now demanding toughened import barriers and other disincentives to the transfer of capital from the United States which could ultimately do more than leftwing governments to reduce the American role in the economic development of the third world.

A second reason why the implications for human-rights diplomacy of our capitalist economic system are obscure is that we are uncertain about the extent to which massive institutionalized violation of human rights is necessary to the preservation of existing, neo-capitalist economic structures. At least in countries like Korea, Singapore, and Taiwan, where a majority of the population participates in the benefits of rapid economic growth, repression may either be residual, obsolete, a reflection merely of competition between elites (rather than classes), and/or a function of a genuinely perceived external threat.

In the third place, leftwing pessimism, resting as it does on a vulgarized simplification of Marx, overlooks the legitimating function of the human-rights campaign. Equating capitalism with freedom powerfully buttresses the former.

When self-styled Marxist governments stifle elementary freedoms, they confirm the proposed equation. It is conversely threatened by the delinquencies of rightwing governments marching under the capitalist banner, even extolling the libertarian virtues of "free enterprise." In exemplifying the possible coexistence, if not the enthusiastic collaboration, of a capitalist economic system and a brutish political order, such governments inflict more ideological injury on the capitalist cause than the venomous polemics of its avowed Marxist enemies. So an evenhanded, humanitarian approach may be attractive to conservatives as a means for strengthening both domestic capitalism (in its struggle against the sort of democratic socialism covertly espoused by populists and left liberals) and the United States in its competitive relations with the Soviet Union.

But its attractions to enlightened conservatives could prove evanescent, resting as they do on the hope that democracy and the capitalist growth model will not prove incompataible in most of the third world. Once a widespread and enduring incompatibility were generally recognized, human rights would be seen to threaten both the ideological and material interests of international capitalism. For any campaign on their behalf would then focus attention on the incompatibility and, to the extent it was successful in opening up political systems, would release forces propelling governments towards socialist development models.

The degree and incidence of injury to capitalist interests in the United States resulting from a change in growth models is unclear. At a minimum, the change would hurt corporations supplying luxury consumer goods to third-world elites, since socialist regimes would tend to reduce the income disparities which enable the upper classes to maintain living standards comparable to those enjoyed by the vast middle classes in affluent countries. Moreover, by decommercializing the communications media—that is, by barring their use to predetermine consumer preference—socialist regimes would lower the profit margins of companies that rely heavily on the creation of consumer preference for brand names through advertising. This would adversely affect a number of multinational corporations based in the United States. Furthermore, by favoring agricultural production for local consumption rather than for export, they would reduce foreign-exchange earnings and thereby possibly jeopardize their capacity to service loans from the private sector in the United States and to permit the repatriation of income earned by local subsidiaries of United States corporations. This change in orientation would not, however, necessarily injure agricultural exports from the United States because demand for food products, released by the redistribution of income to the hungry, might far outstrip the growth of local production.

For my immediate purposes, it is unnecessary to explore all the possible implications of a change in development models. The assumption that any socialist model is undesirable for the national interest shapes United States foreign policy. That assumption has deep and, at least in the short run, seemingly unshakable roots. And so the odds against continued prominence for human rights in the foreign policy of the United States will narrow if there is a slump in confidence about the compatibility of human rights and third-world capitalism.

Human Rights and The Capitalist Growth Model: Are They Compatible?

If we were to imagine the future as a mere extension of the present, confidence in their compatibility would collapse overnight. In many, perhaps most of the capitalist third-world states, economic growth (where it has occurred) has coincided with palpable aggravation of inequality, and in some cases, probably even absolute declines in living standards for the lowest quintiles of the population.

The impact of capitalist development on the exercise of political and civil rights is somewhat more varied, although far from promising. Anything resembling representative government is rare. However, regimes differ significantly in the extent of their tolerance of organizational activity and particularly in their respect for the most basic right, the right of physical security. In other words, the extent of human rights delinquencies seems more a function of noneconomic factors—for example, racial antagonism, the supreme leader's paranoia, or the incompetence or indiscipline of security forces, among other things—than of tensions directly traceable to elite affluence and mass misery. But these variations occur within limits which, with rare exceptions, fall far short of human-rights norms codified in international agreements and declarations. In most countries the polarization generated by inequality seems to insure persistent violation, particularly of the associational and participatory rights of the working and marginalized classes.

Confidence nevertheless survives because of the anticipated transience of radical inequality and the tensions it produces. This happy anticipation stems in turn from the assumption that the developing nations will replicate the historical experience of advanced industrial nations, an experience marked by the coincidence of rapid industrialization and social injustice during the so-called "take-off" period, extending from the last decades of the eighteenth century to the middle of the nineteenth and then, after a period of stable inequality, by a gradual narrowing of income differentials. Even before income differentials narrowed, the vastly increased national wealth trickled down sufficiently to raise living standards. A rising floor under extreme poverty and slowly moderated inequality created a climate of mass accommodation in which a progressively more democratic politics could flourish.

Gripped by this scenario, many Western economists find no grounds for pessimism in the worsening distribution of income. On the contrary, as typified by so respectable a spokesman as Harry Johnson, they affirmatively endorse the laissez-faire attitude of southern governments:

There is likely to be a conflict between rapid growth and an equitable distribution of income; and a poor country anxious to develop would probably be well advised not to worry too much about the distribution of income.[6]

Critics of the conventional extrapolation from the European and American experiences cite differences in economics, politics, technology, ideology, and demographics which, in their judgment, are likely to sustain Disraeli's two nations of the affluent and the impoverished in most developing capitalist states.[7] The lot of the lower classes in Europe and North America began to improve, it is argued, in part because they were absorbed en masse into the work force. As labor became scarce, competition for its services inevitably drove wages up. The scarcity of labor was, in turn, a function of a comparatively gradual increase in the population and a labor-intensive technology. By becoming better paid, better fed, and more valuable to the entrepreneurial class, workers no doubt found it easier to form trade unions, which increased labor's bargaining power both in the market place and in the political arena.

Internal rivalries, nationalist ambitions, enlightened self-interest, and ideology (assuming it is not a wholly dependent variable) moderated capitalist resistance to these developments. The great capitalist entrepreneurs came from outside the traditional landed aristocracy and, after quickly ascending to comparable, often superior economic heights, challenged the old ruling class for political primacy. Their rivalry impeded formation of a common front against the lower classes, even encouraged them to call in new classes of voters to swell the ranks of their respective supporters. Of course, in degrees varying from one country to another, they integrated and cooperated, particularly when faced with a serious threat from the "dangerous classes." But they did not succeed in forming a monolithic opposition to the emancipation and politicization of the working class and the coincidental mitigation of its poverty.

Rivalry was only one reason. Self-interest also played a role. The means of repression were primitive, little more efficient in most respects than those available in earlier centuries. Lacking that degree of repressive power which produces almost effortless intimidation, repression unalloyed with elements of accommodation would have been costly, even dangerous. There was a more positive kind of self-interest as well. This was a real concordance of interest between capital and labor stemming from the principal threat to profits and stability: insufficient demand for the plethora of goods spilling out of the new industrial cornucopia. More perceptive capitalists grasped the elementary point that workers with money were consumers.

Nationalist ambitions—a symbiotic mingling of capitalist and aristocratic lusts reinforced by a half-literate mass's appetite for vicarious achievement—reinforced the will to accommodate. Repression might do if the working masses were required only as cannon fodder in the struggle for economic growth. But if the masses were to be fodder for real cannons in the struggle for military victory over other nationally organized elites, they had first to feel a higher alliance to their kith and kin, regardless of class, than to the other workers of the world. They had, in short, to be integrated into the political nation. A liberal political ideology already widely diffused at the very outset of the industrial revolution encouraged and facilitated mass participation in national politics.

If these were the essential features of Western society's evolution from the grim beginnings of the Industrial Revolution to the modern welfare state, only blind faith, it is argued, can support optimism about comparable developments in the capitalist nations of the third world. A demographic explosion couples with a capital-intensive technology, conceived in labor-scarce states, to maintain a ballooning reserve army of under- and unemployed. In many countries, and particularly in Latin America, capitalist entrepreneurs and managers either come from, are co-opted into, or are dominated by the traditional classes. Where the upper classes are not fused into a single homogeneous elite, they nevertheless generally prefer collaboration to rivalry. And in their unremitting efforts to block the organization of a mass generally less literate and more incoherent and disoriented than its European predecessors, they deploy means of repression beyond the dreams of nineteenth-century capitalists.

While repression is cheaper and its victims more expendable, there are no countervailing economic incentives for accommodation. In many countries, national poverty is less a function of insufficient local demand than an absolute deficiency in the means for producing goods and services. Nor do national rivalries seem to play the same kind of accommodating role they once filled. Whether because of a heightened sense of common class interest, or the declining legitimacy of and growing costs of war, or for other reasons, national capitalist elites evince reduced antagonism and a correspondingly greater capacity for cooperation, particularly in suppressing challenges to their hegemony.

Though all of this makes up a strong case for pessimism, at this point it is possible to remain wistfully agnostic. The case possibly exaggerates certain differences between the European and the third-world setting and does not take entirely convincing account of such new factors as the egalitarian ideology which seems to have displaced the nineteenth century's reigning emphasis on individual autonomy. Another new factor is the capacity of the state apparatus, particularly in the more advanced developing countries, to accumulate and invest capital; growth is no longer at the mercy of the marginal propensity of the rich to save. Yet another novel factor, rich in unpredictable implications, is the emergence of the military as an independent social group with passions, interests, and ambitions which are not invariably congruent with those of the monied classes.

Although the domestic and foreign policy risks are real, they should not deter this or any other Administration from making a real national effort to promote human rights. For I believe that if we can persist, a larger number of the middle-class states of the third world will enter the stage of high technology as democracies linked to the liberal West. Ideology has its momentum too. If authoritarian solutions to the problems of class and ethnic conflict, alienation, terrorism, inflation, and unemployment, which plague societies at many levels of development, become the norm throughout the southern hemisphere and the ranks of the democracies consequently do not swell, they may dwindle.

The problem is not simply one of a contagion of ideas among elites. Just as the defenders of freedom feel threatened by powerful foreign enemies of the open society, so the authoritarians who rely on our good will are threatened by the existence of a liberal and democratic America which will shelter their enemies, condemn their barbarities, and, by its very existence, will challenge their view that capitalism requires the suspension of freedom. Hence they are bound to support forces in our own society infirmly committed to democratic institutions. And so in the process of saving lives in far-off places, we may help to save those features of our own society which deserve the good opinion of mankind.

NOTES

1. James P. Grant, *Disparity Reduction Rates In Social Indicators* (Washington, D.C.: Overseas Development Council, 1978), p. 7.
2. Figures are taken from the Grant monograph.
3. Grant, op. cit., p. 33.
4. Ibid., p. 34.

5. Since the Iranian revolution does not seem to have demolished the administration's tip-toeing efforts to promote human rights, perhaps we should somewhat discount this concern.
6. Harry Johnson, *Money, Trade and Economic Growth* (Cambridge, Harvard U. Press 1967).
7. The single most penetrating and subtle statement of the pessimistic hypothesis which I have seen is Sylvia Hewlett's "Human Rights and Economic Realities in Developing Countries," to be published in *The Future of the Inter-American System,* Tom Farer, ed., New York: (Praeger, 1979). I have relied very heavily on it in the following summary of the extrapolation's critics.

Domestic Politics
Behind
Human Rights Diplomacy

SANDY VOGELGESANG

I have a dream that one day this nation will rise up and live out the true meaning of its creed; "We hold these truths to be self-evident that all men are created equal."

Martin Luther King

Jimmy Carter did not invent the concept of human rights. It reflects the very roots of the republic. What he did signal, with his inaugural address in 1977, was the culmination of changes inside the United States that, in turn, may lead to a new era for its foreign policy. A look at the record—the historical backdrop and the period between 1973 and 1978—reveals the often decisive domestic dimension of human rights diplomacy. Indeed, the thrust of argument here is that domestic political considerations constitute the overriding factor behind the emphasis of the United States on human rights abroad. To that end, this discussion addresses the past, or the background of the American tradition, the present, or the reasons for the recent revival of interest in human rights, and the future, the implications of changes in the 1970s.[1]

49

THE HISTORICAL BACKDROP

The history of American domestic reaction to human rights, at home and abroad, helps Americans see themselves more as others do and put the more recent policy of the United States into perspective. Americans pride themselves with considerable justification, on a dream which they hope may become the destiny of all. Yet, there is sometimes a darker side to their expressed ideals. As the following brief illustrative survey suggests, clearing away the national rhetoric can bring to light a discrepancy between desires and actions.

First, there has been a recurrent discrepancy between public opinion and official deed. At various times, presidents of the United States have either ignored public pressure for intervention abroad in order to protect what they saw as the broader national interest or fought in vain to rouse Americans to react against the abrogation of rights elsewhere. For example, George Washington coolly resisted the public clamor to support the French Revolution. In contrast, Woodrow Wilson and Franklin Delano Roosevelt failed to mobilize public backing for efforts designed to make the world safe for democracy.

Second, there has been a discrepancy between what Americans say about human rights and their actual intent in advocating these rights. For instance, Latin American leaders interpreted the Monroe Doctrine correctly: It was less for the sake of their freedom, than for the promotion of the economic and strategic interests of the United States.

Third, politicians in the United States have not hesitated to promote human rights for their own political advantage. Although Theodore Roosevelt claimed that his "cowboy diplomacy" in Central America was based on what he called "a mandate from civilization," it served what may well have been the more central purpose: It helped put him before the public eye and into the White House. Domestic political considerations also have helped explain the concern Americans seem to express about the plight of Jews in the Soviet Union.

Fourth, there have been some conspicuous lapses in the support of human rights abroad that have undercut the credibility of the concern. Much of the diplomacy of the United States in Central America and the Caribbean has made a mockery of its expressed dedication to self-determination. When the United States sent Marines to quell the liberal opposition in Nicaragua in the 1920s, one member of Congress asked: "Oh, Monroe Doctrine, how many crimes have been committed in thy name?"

Fifth, there have been lapses in the advocacy of human rights in the United States itself. Foreign critics of the Carter administration's emphasis on human rights dwell on what they see as the hypocrisy of American diplomacy. They point out, in that regard, the fact that the Founding Fathers held slaves and that Abraham Lincoln suspended the writ of habeas corpus. Of more recent concern, they observe that blacks and whites were pushed into prisons with cattle prods for seeking voter registration in the American South during the 1960s and that the United States has yet to ratify major international documents on human rights or an Equal Rights Amendment for its female majority.

THE RECENT REVIVAL

The politics of human rights is the domestic counterpart of the diplomacy of human rights.[2] It calls the key politicians in the United States into play: the President, the Congress, the public, and special interest groups. And, it serves as many purposes as there are protagonists. It can be as notable for making Americans feel better about themselves, as for actually improving the lot of the victims of human-rights violations. This section addresses some reasons for the new emphasis on human rights during the 1970s, the role of the more important people involved, and some constraints on stressing human rights.

A Convergence of Concerns

The issue of human rights came to the fore in the 1970s largely due to the congruence of several disparate developments. The most significant among them were domestic reaction against the involvement of the United States in Vietnam, the spillover from the American civil rights movement, the domestic response to particular political events around the world, and changes within the Congress and in relations between the legislative and executive branches of the United States government.

The disenchantment of Americans with the Indochina conflict was, of all those factors, probably preeminent. Whether seen as an example of executive excess, a distortion of national interest, or an instance of American moralism run amok, domestic disquiet over that experience set the stage for stress on human rights in the foreign policy of the United States. Reaction against the Vietnam War might have spurred just the opposite effect. Disgust with the distortion of expressed democratic goals in Indochina could have caused more Americans to look inward and resist other efforts to apply their values elsewhere. Instead, that sentiment helped create a moral vacuum and the need to fill it with restored self-respect. Further, one of the more interesting aspects of the human-rights issue is the large number of proponents who were once either activists in the civil rights movement, or opponents of the involvement of the United States in Southeast Asia, or both. For example, Representative Tom Harkin (Democrat of Iowa) traces his commitment to human rights to the discovery, while a Congressional staff member, of South Vietnam's "tiger cages" for prisoners. Since his election to Congress in 1974, Harkin has been a prime mover behind much human-rights legislation.

Political developments around the world in the late 1960s and 1970s helped attract even more attention to the human rights question and—most to the point of American political concern—the alleged role of the United States in that repression. Exposés of misconduct by the Central Intelligence Agency, as well as the close support by the United States for dictatorial governments such as those of Park Chung-hee in South Korea and Ferdinand Marcos in the Philippines, gave Americans a sense of hypocrisy on human rights. This feeling was increased when it was asserted that the United States ousted Salvador Allende's Marxist but democratically elected government in Chile and supported the subsequent military junta. Promotion of détente, at the apparent expense of freedom for Soviet and Eastern European dissidents, increasing investment by American companies in countries such as South Africa, and charges that the United States government had helped train foreign internal security forces intensified the demand for human rights.

Reports on these developments coincided with a related shift within the United States government. In the 1970s the political power needed to effect the foreign policy of the United States shifted from the

White House to the other end of Pennsylvania Avenue. Vietnam and Watergate had helped shatter the image of the White House concerning foreign policy. Questions about policy toward the Greek junta raised by the 1974 Cyprus crisis, anger about allegedly limited congressional-executive consultations on events in Angola in 1975, and concern about negotiations for bases in Spain and the Philippines were—in addition to revelations noted above—among other developments that fostered Congressional disillusionment. More and more members of Congress wondered whether they could trust the executive branch to take effective action on foreign policy. More often than not, their answer was no.

The Congress thus moved to assume a larger role in the formation and implementation of foreign policy. As a result, the War Powers Act of 1973 was passed over President Nixon's veto to restrain the power of the President to commit armed forces abroad; the Clark Amendment of 1975 was enacted to ban future aid to factions in Angola's civil war; and an amendment to the Arms Export Control Act of 1975 was made that required any sale of military equipment totaling over $7 million to rest 60 days in the Congress before becoming final. Finally, more stress was placed on human rights. The Jackson-Vanik Amendment to the Trade Act of 1974 was passed to permit Congressmen to participate in more decisions about foreign policy, including that policy which could affect human rights.[3]

Although the times were ripe for stressing human rights, the issue's sudden salience owes much to the action, reaction, and interaction between two individuals. Henry Kissinger, then the Secretary of State was an advocate of *Realpolitik*. Donald Fraser, then a little-known Congressman from Minnesota, launched the hearings that laid the basis for a challenge to Kissinger's view of

American foreign policy and to eventual legislation on human rights. First, in 1973 Kissinger gave an address before the "Pacem in Terris" Conference, October 8. In the meantime, he testified before the Subcommittee on International Organizations and Movements of the Committee on Foreign Affairs between August 1 and December 7. Kissinger's speech set forth the perspectives on the role of human rights in the foreign policy of the United States which were to govern his subsequent actions as Secretary.[4] His dominant concern in 1973 and thereafter was for the policy-maker to strike a "balance between what is desirable and what is possible." After stating that "America cannot be true to itself without moral purpose," Kissinger cautioned:

> When policy becomes excessively moralistic, it may turn quixotic or dangerous. A presumed monopoly on truth obstructs negotiation and accommodation. Good results may be given up in the quest for ever elusive ideal solution. Policy may fall prey to intellectual posturing or adventuristic crusades.

He was to elaborate on human rights in 1977: "It was under the banners of moralistic slogans a decade and a half ago that we launched adventures that divided our country and undermined our international position."

There were several other general arguments that underlay Kissinger's position on human rights. He believed that the legitimate function of foreign policy was to deal, one nation to another, on the basis of external conduct. (Critics would argue that Kissinger's conduct vis-à-vis the Allende government in Chile and elsewhere belied that belief.) Lapsing into discussion of internal matters could put the United States on a slippery slope—with spokesmen for the United States voicing hollow rhetoric

or veering toward intervention. It also posed the dilemma of a double standard, given different leverage
for the United States on different situations and the
genuine security threat before some nations. Any reference to human rights, however, should be made quietly
since he believed that governments do not respond posi-
tively to public assault.

Peace itself was, according to Kissinger, a moral objective. Pursuit of a SALT agreement, resolution of the
Mideast crisis, and the "opening to China" were aspects
of that effort which the secretary thought might be undercut by a campaign on human rights. He defined a
statesman as someone willing to be unpopular and to
take the long view, to have a vision of the national interest. That interpretation of the national interest put preeminent stress on world order and stability, on security
derived from balance among the major global powers,
and on the need for flexibility for the executive branch
to fulfill national needs and aspirations. Kissinger believed that the Congress should stay out of the day-to-
day details of diplomacy. The legislators should not, as
one former Kissinger aide described the secretary's
view, "hamstring his pursuit of the national interest."

However, it was primarily growing Congressional criticism of Kissinger by the mid-1970s—some of which
concerned his attitude towards human rights—that
forced the secretary to pay more attention to the Constitutional and political need for a congressional role in
foreign policy. As a result, Congressman Fraser, concerned by what he considered previously "random" and
"unpredictable" Congressional attention to human
rights, was able to organize, with the help of committee
staff member John Salzberg, a series of 15 hearings.
They were a conscious effort to educate Capitol Hill, the
executive branch, and the country on human rights.

The summary report from those hearings struck a tone diametrically opposed to that expressed by Kissinger. It stressed that:

> The human rights factor is not accorded the high priority it deserves in our country's foreign policy. Too often it becomes invisible on the vast foreign policy horizon of political, economic and military affairs.
>
> An increasingly interdependent world means that disregard for human rights in one country can have repercussions in others. . . . Consideration for human rights in foreign policy is both morally imperative and practically necessary.[5]

Conclusions from the Fraser hearings suggested both a different reading of the moral and legal commitments of the United States and a divergent view of how respect for human rights could affect short- and long-term interests of the United States—whether judged by changing domestic support for American foreign policy or repercussions abroad. And, there was the unspoken assertion that Congress had a particular responsibility to speak out to adjust an alleged distortion in Executive Branch perspective, and thus to accord more closely with values expressed in the Constitution and Bill of Rights. That is, the hearings required government officials to support the cause of human rights. They built a considerable record of testimony from government officials, representatives of nongovernmental organizations, members of the Congress, and scholars; they also laid the basis for recommendations raising the priority given to human rights in foreign policy and strengthening the capacity of international organizations to further human rights.

Fraser followed up on those hearings by writting letters to the Department of State on human rights.[6] Subsequent hearings on individual countries eventually brought explicit legislation on human rights.[7]

Section 32 of the Foreign Assistance Act of 1973 made a *tentative* beginning to assure human rights were given priority in legislation: "It is the sense of Congress that the President should deny any economic or military assistance to the government of any foreign country which practices the internment or imprisonment of that country's citizens for political purposes." The executive promptly convinced the Congress that such legislation presented difficulties of definition which, in turn, made implementation impossible. Although that legislation, aimed at the government of South Vietnam, proved impractical, it did lead to the exchange of a series of letters between then Deputy Secretary of State Robert Ingersoll and Thomas Morgan, Chairman of the House International Relations Committee (HIRC). In that correspondence, the department noted its support for human rights considerations in foreign policy and began what amounted to institutionalization of this concern within the State Department bureaucracy.[8] On April 4, 1974, the Department of State asked United States embassies in 68 countries receiving assistance to report on their treatment of political prisoners. Those requests for information were later expanded to include respect for the full range of human rights. Information about the content of Section 32 was brought to the attention of governments in the East Asian and Pacific region. Kissinger, while opposed to explicit rebukes in his own name to foreign governments, would and did clear cables that conveyed the critical "mood of Congress" on human rights.

The Congress, while taking the lead on human rights

in general and in the use of economic sanctions to guarantee them in particular, also tried a *positive,* as well as a more punitive, approach. Here, too, Congressman Fraser played a central role. It was he who was largely responsible for the fundamental reevaluation of foreign assistance from the United States in the early 1970s. Given the scope of the United Nations Universal Declaration of Human Rights (which includes economic and social rights, as well as political and civil liberties) and growing concern that economic development in the third world was not trickling down to the poor, he helped lead the successful congressional campaign to establish "new directions" for development assistance from the United States. The congruence of events— between the new directions legislation of 1973 that mandated stress on meeting the basic human needs of the poor and the previously mentioned Section 32 of the Foreign Assistance Act with its restrictions on assistance—was not by coincidence, nor without consequence.[9]

Timing continued to work to the advantage of human-rights advocates. In 1974 there was a growing confrontation between the executive branch and Congress over many issues. The off-year elections brought to Washington many antiwar congressmen—including Tom Harkins. Even before the election, members of the Congress had become more and more troubled by inadequate respect for human rights in countries receiving assistance from the United States. Thus, on September 20, 1974, Congressman Fraser delivered to Secretary Kissinger a letter signed by 105 members of the Congress. They stated that their support for future legislation on foreign aid would be influenced by the extent to which American foreign policy showed more concern for human rights in recipient countries. Since many members of the Congress believed that the executive branch had ignored their concern about human rights, expressed in 1973, they added a new section to the Foreign Assistance Act of 1974. Section 502B stated the sense of the Congress that, "except in extraordinary circumstances, the President shall substantially reduce or terminate security assistance to any government which engaged in a consistent pattern of gross violations of internationally recognized human rights." The president was to advise Congress of extenuating circumstances which might necessitate sending security assistance to any government engaging in such violations of human rights.

The State Department reportedly had planned to respond by submitting to Congress analyses of how prospective aid recipients handled human rights and why security requirements dictated continued aid. Although State Department officials knew that supporters of human rights in Congress welcomed preliminary steps taken in behalf of human rights during the previous year, they still believed that response to Section 502B would constitute a critical test of the intent of the executive branch. Senators Edward Kennedy, Alan Cranston, and others had made clear that they were looking for the reduction or elimination of security assistance in serious problem cases and/or persuasive evidence that the State Department was actively pursuing other measures to foster human rights.[10]

The executive branch failed that test. Secretary Kissinger decided that making reports concerning human rights in countries receiving security assistance would harm the conduct of the foreign policy of the United States. Thus, although the department, under the direction of Carlyle Maw (then the Under Secretary for Security Assistance and personal lawyer for the secretary), had supervised the preparation of these reports, the Department did not submit them to the Congress. Instead, it provided what congressional analysts considered "a bland unsigned summary report" to the Senate Foreign Relations Committee. That report concluded that neither the security interests of the United States nor the cause of human rights would be served by the "public obloquy and impaired relations with security assistance recipient countries" that would follow necessarily subjective determinations on human rights conditions and that "quiet but forceful diplomacy" is the best way to further respect for human rights.[11]

Both Senator Cranston and Congressman Fraser rejected the State Department's contention that no objective means existed to make distinctions among offending nations. Cranston replied, "There may be no objective way to determine the degree of violations, but does the Secretary of State have any subjective feelings about what is going on in Chile, Brazil, Korea, Indonesia, Ethiopia, and the Philippines today?"[12] Kissinger seemed to treat Congress as an irrelevant interference with his own prerogatives on foreign policy. According to his critics, the European-born statesman did not appreciate American values and institutions and reflected that cynical disregard when he thumbed his nose at the American system of checks and balances.

Frustration with the "Kissinger Administration," augmented by increased congressional concern about specific atrocities committed by the Chilean *junta* and what Congress considered an inadequate response by the executive branch to more general repression throughout Latin America, thus colored consideration of human-rights legislation in 1975 and 1976. The International Development and Food Assistance Act of 1975 amended a bill from the previous year to:

—Provide that economic assistance may not be given to any country which consistently violates international recognized human rights;
—Require the President to submit to Congress a written report explaining how assistance would directly benefit the people of such a country;
—Stipulate that, if either house of Congress disagrees with the President's justification, it may take action to terminate economic assistance to that country by a concurrent resolution.

Gone was the loose language reflecting the "sense of the Congress." Angry at what many considered Kissinger's callous disregard for congressional concerns, the legislators had moved to make the *first mandatory* restrictions on aid from the United States—on human-rights grounds.

Significant as this move was, it did stop short of the possible complete cutoff sought by Congressman Harkin and Senator James Abourezk (Democrat of South Dakota). The 1975 bill carried the proviso that aid might still be given to a repressive regime, *if* that assistance directly benefited the "needy people" in the country in question. What cynics soon tagged the "needy people loophole" resulted from arguments by the congressional leadership that legislation on security assistance was a more appropriate means for promoting human rights than was development aid. HIRC Chairman Morgan, supported by Fraser, helped deflect congressional anger from a course that could have put strong constraints on the AID program.

The Congress instead focused its attention on security

assistance. The first draft of a bill in that area, done in late 1975, reflected a predictably strong position vis-à-vis the executive branch. Although the State Department tried to work with congressional staff members on a compromise, little was given on human rights. Fraser had the full backing of HIRC Chairman Morgan. Senators Humphrey, Case, and Javits supported Cranston. When President Ford vetoed the 1976 authorization, in May, with the explanation that it raised "fundamental constitutional problems" and "would seriously inhibit my ability to implement a coherent and consistent foreign policy," the Congress came back with another version. The result was Section 301 of the International Security Assistance and Arms Export Control Act (PL 94-329, approved on June 30, 1976). Prepared against the backdrop of the previous winter of Congressional displeasure, it provided for the following:

—Established within the State Department a Coordinator for Human Rights and Humanitarian Affairs to be appointed by the President with the advice and consent of the Senate;
—Required the Secretary of State to submit reports each fiscal year on human rights practices in each country proposed as a recipient of security assistance;
—Required upon request of either the House or Senate or of either foreign relations committee that the Secretary of State prepare, with the assistance of the Coordinator, a statement on a designated country's human rights practices;
—Established that, if such a statement on a designated country is not transmitted within 30 days, security assistance to that country will cease until the statement is transmitted;

—Provided that, after the requested statement is transmitted, Congress may reduce or end security assistance to that designated country by adoption of a joint resolution.

This 1976 incarnation of the Foreign Assistance Act was the culmination of a long struggle, marked by increasing congressional frustration with resistance and, sometimes, obstruction from the executive branch to legislative initiatives on human rights. Therein lay the cause for Kissinger's growing concern. The Congress had enacted provisions targetted at particular countries, including South Korea, Chile, the Soviet Union, and Uruguay. Legislation adopted in mid-1976 required the executive directors appointed by the United States to the Inter-American Development Bank and the African Development Fund to vote against loans to countries where the governments seriously violated human rights.

Fear that such international financial institutions might become what some officials at the departments of State and the Treasury called "the cutting edge of the human rights crusade" prompted increased, albeit belated, attention by the Ford Administration to both human rights and consultations with the Congress on that subject. Charles Robinson, then Deputy Secretary of State, met with Senator Cranston and Congressman Fraser on July 22, 1976. Robinson was impressed by his meeting with the congressmen, encouraged by his immediate staff, and prompted by his own personal concern about human rights. He therefore asked the department's Policy Planning Staff to formulate criteria for more thoughtful and consistent implementation of human-rights provisions in existing legislation. Time, however, was to run out on that effort—and for the Ford administration.

The Transition

By late 1976, interaction between the executive branch and the Congress on human rights had achieved several results. Congressional advocates of human rights had made those in the ranks of the bureaucracy aware of the issue, if not those ·at the highest reaches of the administration. Indeed, human rights emerged as a more conspicuous theme in Kissinger's speeches in the election year. His address before the Synagogue Council of America (October 19, 1976) was influenced by an appreciation for the sensitivities of the audience, growing congressional interest in human righs—and the fact that then presidential candidate Jimmy Carter had made a strong human rights speech before the Convention of B'nai B'rith on September 8, 1976. Congressional pressure influenced Kissinger's speech before the Sixth General Assembly of the Organization of American States in Santiago, Chile, June 6, 1976. Congressional interest, together with what was an even more compelling concern for new geopolitical developments in Africa, influenced Kissinger's major shift in 1976 toward support for majority rule in southern Africa.

Inside the State Department, the bureaucracy wrestled over what to make of pronouncements in the presidential campaign and existing legislation. First, draft papers on human rights, prepared at the request of the Carter transition team during December 1976 and January 1977, tended to play down "the problem with Congress." However, officers from several bureaus throughout the State Department did question analysis which they believed would either distort the actual attitude of congressmen or lack credibility for the new administration. They stressed that congressional insistence on legislation illustrated mistrust of the motives of the executive branch. It would be a mistake to dismiss the movement—spearheaded by Senators Kennedy and Cranston and Representatives Fraser, Koch, and Harkin—as a "small band of extremists." They thought that a sizeable majority in the Congress believed that the United States should distance itself publicly from repressive regimes to demonstrate disfavor for the violations of human rights. These officials concluded by advocating that the State Department work with, not against, the Congress to find constructive ways to promote human rights.

Just as State Department officials were preparing for a new way to deal with human rights—and the Congress—so were many on Capitol Hill reviewing strategy. Members and their staffs gathered frequently in late 1976. Many had been flattered by the attention showered on them earlier in the year by campaigners for Jimmy Carter. The fact that the Carter people had taken time to elicit their views stood in marked contrast to what they considered the "cold shoulder" from the Ford administration. (Such efforts were to lay the basis for much subsequent collaboration, officially and unofficially, on human rights.) Most acknowledged, according to later interviews with many of the participants, the need to work with the new administration on human rights. Some even conceded the "one-sided" nature of some congressional hearings on human rights and admitted that some legislation was enacted more as a reaction against the "Lone Ranger" style of Henry Kissinger, than as the best means to further human rights. Most believed that Kissinger's exit opened the door to a new, more positive attitude at the State Department toward human rights. They welcomed the arrival of a new generation of officials, not molded by the pressures of the Cold War or McCarthyite attacks in the 1950s. The transition period ended with Congressional advocates of human rights wondering about themselves and their prospective counterparts in the executive branch. Might an excess of zeal jeopardize the cause for years to come?

Campaign pledges on behalf of human rights set the initial tone for the new Carter administration. In his inaugural address, the President stressed: "Our moral sense dictates a clearcut preference for those societies which share with us an abiding respect for individual human rights." This section provides detailed description of some early actions by the Carter administration and the Congress—and interaction between the two branches of the government—to illustrate the special domestic political dynamics behind the human rights issue.

Senior spokesmen for the Carter administration moved quickly to distance themselves from Kissinger's alleged disdain for human rights and to establish their own *bona fides* on the subject. Both the president and the secretary of state stressed that concern for human rights should be "a fundamental factor" in the formulation and implementation of American foreign policy. Consideration for human rights was to pervade bilateral relations with other nations and such issues as arms transfer and the north-south dialogue, a point stressed in the Presidential Review Memoranda of the new administration. In that way, American diplomacy would, as press guidance for the State Department suggested, reflect traditional national values and legal commitments.

To help gain congressional confidence in the administration's commitment to human rights, the State Department's Bureau of Congressional Relations recommended that senior-level officials meet with congressional advocates of human rights. Leaders in the field, such as Fraser and Kennedy, were to be consulted on how to implement the Administration's human-rights policy. There was particular concern about reassuring the congressmen on the seriousness of intent of the executive branch, drawing out their ideas, and discussing the need for certain security assistance programs. That bureau also encouraged the Secretary to meet with members of the congressional black caucus, in accordance with their request. It did so on the grounds that that group could help the administration develop human rights criteria, that it could facilitate administration objectives in Africa, and that three such meetings held over the previous 18 months with Kissinger had proved useful.

In addition to such informal meetings with members of the Congress, there was a full roster of appearances by senior spokesmen for the Carter administration before congressional committees. Each presentation in early 1977 was considered a crucial effort to set a new tone and meet the Congress more than half way. The administration complemented these statements with actions, such as cuts in security assistance to some repressive governments. More to the point at hand, the administration acted quickly in 1977 to test and confirm the sincerity of congressional resolve on human rights. In a notable display of good timing, the White House sought and got congressional repeal of the Byrd Amendment. It thus restored a complete boycott on Rhodesian goods just before the president's maiden speech in the United Nations. In that address (March 17, 1977), Carter announced his intention to seek Senate advice and consent for ratification of major covenants and conventions on human rights. The president stressed in a speech before the O.A.S. Permanent Council (April 14, 1977) his intention to seek Senate approval for ratification of the American Convention on Human Rights.

Congress responded, for several reasons, by continuing to press promotion of human rights. Mistrust of the
executive branch persisted after the Kissinger period.
Jimmy Carter, many thought, had yet to establish his
credentials on human rights. Other congressional advocates of human rights were jealous when the executive
branch *did* show interest in the subject and thus wanted
to accelerate their own campaign. And according to mail
from constituents and public opinion polls at the time
human rights remained popular. There was thus considerable congressional activity on human rights in 1977.
In March, both the House and the Senate—sensitive to
the extensive coverage by the press on relations between
the United States and the Soviet Union and the role of
human rights in that relationship—passed, by lop-sided
margins, resolutions to convey the interest of the American people in Soviet adherence to the Helsinki Final
Act. The Subcommittee on Foreign Assistance of the
Senate Foreign Relations Committee, as part of a follow-
up on 1976 legislation, made public a State Department
"report card" on human rights conditions in 82 nations.
Congressman Fraser maintained a brisk pace of hearings that included testimony on respect for human
rights in East Timor, Vietnam, Thailand, Cambodia, El
Salvador, and Iran and reviews on attention to human
rights at the 1977 sessions of the United Nations Human
Rights Commission and the O.A.S. General Assembly.

Important as these activities were, action in another
quarter provided the most significnt index to congressional interest in human rights and the relation of Congress to the White House on this issue. Debate raged
throughout much of 1977 over whether to put restrictions on the participation of the United States in *all*
international financial institutions (IFI's). To do so entailed extending the language of the Harkin Amend-

ment, adopted in 1976 for the votes of the United States in the Inter-American Development Bank and the African Development Fund, to such major institutions as the World Bank. The human-rights lobby, eager to make legislative purview in the economic sector as complete as possible, pushed for what its member organizations saw as the necessary next step after restrictions on all bilateral aid and some multilateral assistance by the United States. The result was the reincarnation of "Harkin language" in Title VII of HR 5262. That bill authorized increased capital subscriptions by the United States to the International Bank for Reconstruction and Development, the International Development Association, the International Finance Corporation, the Asian Development Bank, and the Asian Development Fund.

The Carter administration, despite its strong public pitch for human rights, fought hard to defeat this bill and, indeed, to repeal Harkin language elsewhere. Tense discussions ensued between members of the administration and the Congress. The former found themselves in the embarrassing position of arguing for "flexibility"—a warning from the Kissinger period. Congressional advocates of human rights split over that kind of appeal. One group preferred to give the Administration a honeymoon, whereas the other wanted to capitalize on the mounting momentum in behalf of human rights.

The first round went to the human-rights moderates. The administration, after considerable pressure and correspondence from Deputy Secretary of State Warren Christopher and National Security Adviser Zbigniew Brzezinski, agreed to compromise language worked out by Henry Reuss (Democrat of Wisconsin), the chairman of the House Committee on Banking, Currency, and Housing and, traditionally, a strong advocate of human

rights. However, Harkin and Herman Badillo (Democrat of New York) led a successful fight in the House to
restore more rigid human-rights restrictions on the
participation of the United States in the IFI's. James
Abourezk, the blunt one-term senator from South Dakota, led the campaign for Harkin-Badillo language in
the Senate. In one of his last major legislative efforts,
Hubert Humphrey, often using talking points supplied
by the State Department, championed the administration's version of the bill. Abourezk's effort surprised
Humphrey and the administration. It drew on a rare
mix of conservative and liberal support and fell only
seven votes short of passage. House and Senate con-
ferees then conferred for weeks to achieve final compromise. The result was P.L. 95-118, signed into law on
October 3, 1977. Title VII of that bill gave some latitude
to the executive branch, but not as much as the Carter
administration had wanted. The government was to use
"its voice and vote" to advance respect for human rights
in the international financial institutions. Lest the administration lapse from compliance, the departments of
State and the Treasury were to report to the Congress
on their actions. These structures were reiterated in the
act providing appropriations for capital subscriptions
from the United States to the IFI's (P.L. 95-148, October
31, 1977).

Thoughout late 1977 and 1978, human-rights advocates in the Congress continued efforts to extend their
legislative mandate into the economic sector and to
monitor implementation of laws already in effect. Their
efforts did not stop with restrictions on bilateral and
multilateral aid. New legislation included an amendment to the Export-Import Act of 1945, signed into law
on October 26, 1977. This required that the Board of
Directors, in authorizing any loan or guarantee for the

Export-Import Bank "take into account, in consultation with the Secretary of State, the observance of and respect for human rights in the country to receive the exports supported by a loan or financial guarantee and the effect such exports may have on human rights in such country." Also, the Overseas Private Investment Corporation Amendments Act of 1978 was signed into law on April 24, 1978. It amended the Foreign Assistance Act of 1961 so that the Corporation would take into account the status of human rights and the effect of its programs on human rights in countries where OPIC operates. The Bretton Woods Agreements Act was amended to authorize the participation of the United States in the Supplementary Financing Facility (SFF) of the International Monetary Fund (signed into law on October 10, 1978). It carried special provisions on both human rights and human needs. The Executive Director, from the United States, on the Executive Board of the Fund was required to initiate efforts assuring use of SFF funds for "the poor majority." The departments of State and the Treasury were to prepare annual reports on the status of human rights in countries receiving SFF funds. An amendment to the Foreign Assistance Appropriations Act for fiscal year 1979 (Section 611 of Public Law 95-481) was made that stated that the president shall direct those governors from the United States of the International Bank for Reconstruction and Development, the International Finance Corporation, the International Development Association, the Inter-American Development Bank, the Asian Development Bank, and the African Development Fund " to propose and seek adoption of an amendment to the Articles of Agreement for their respective institutions to establish human rights standards to be considered in connection with each application for assistance." Numerous restrictions were placed on transactions with specific countries. For example, Congress has placed various curbs on economic and military assistance to Chile since 1974 because of the alleged violations of human rights by that nation's military junta. The Jackson-Vanik and Stevenson Amendments to the Trade Reform Act were designed to use the leverage of trade and credits to help achieve freer emigration from the Soviet Union and Eastern Europe. Senator Kennedy made a successful effort to cut off arms transfers to Argentina by October, 1978.

For several reasons, the concern for human rights is growing. As a result, legislators have tried to introduce or have succeeded in requiring that human rights be taken into consideration before legislation on foreign economic policy is approved. Many now prefer to see how that legislation might work before making further changes or additions. Others believe, however, that putting restrictions on some multilateral institutions, such as the International Monetary Fund, may not be the most effective means to promote human rights. Second, more and more members of the Congress, confident that they have established their overall commitment to human rights, think that it is time to refine the implementation of foreign policy. For example, many, in partial response to pressure from the business community in the United States and because of increasing consternation about the declining competitiveness of American exports, want to back off from proposals, such as that advocating complete restrictions on operations of the Export-Import Bank. That, they suspect, may be "too blunt an instrument," one that hurts American business without alleviating the human-rights problems of most concern to most Americans. There is thus a trend toward identifying those countries where, in the view of the Congress, the human-rights situation is most objectionable and/or where the United States can do something about it or should, at the least, make its opposition known.

South Africa is one of the nations that has attracted special congressional interest. Given the apparent intransigence of the Afrikaners and the special sensitivity of Americans to racial discrimination, Congress has begun to add more stringent economic sanctions to the other restrictions (such as the United Nations mandatory arms embargo) already in effect. Language attached in 1978 to the continuing authorization for Exim operations prohibits, for example, Exim guarantees for exports to the South African Government and its agencies and provides financing to private companies only if they adhere to a code of principles intended to help eliminate apartheid. Attempts, so far unsuccessful, to prohibit all new investment in South Africa by multinational corporations or to deny tax credits to companies doing business in South Africa, are likely to be made again.

Momentum Behind the Movement

By the late 1970s, the issue of human rights had taken on a life of its own. It did so—partly because of those factors already noted which lay behind the emergence of the issue in the early 1970s and partly because of particular domestic political considerations.

Carter's arrival in the White House provided the most significant new prod to promotion of human rights, placing the power and prestige of the White House behind human rights, which, before, had been primarily supported by Congress. There was a greater range of action open to the executive branch and the president

could command more attention from the press and
media. Further, had Gerald Ford won the 1976 election
and had he continued, as seemed likely, the same substance and style of foreign policy, human rights would
probably have remained more of a bone of domestic
contention along Pennsylvania Avenue than a subject of
international interest.

Jimmy Carter, the man, proved crucial to the new
turn to human rights. Although the emphasis on human
rights resulted, in part, from the findings of Patrick
Caddell, Carter's adviser on public opinion, and the
urgings of his campaign staff, Carter himself strongly
believed in the cause. He considered it important that
political and personal values coincide. Thus, his earnest
report to a convention of fellow Southern Baptists in
1978: "I have never detected or experienced any conflict
between God's will and my political duty." Fortunately
for Carter, values could be translated into votes. Astute
politician that he was, he seized on that opportunity.
Whether seeking the support of the nation's 26 million
Baptists or the less numerous Jews (albeit concentrated
in several swing states), he made clear during the presidential campaign that the suffering of religious dissidents in the Soviet Union " will be very much on my
mind when I negotiate with the Soviet Union and you
can depend on that."[13]

Although advocacy of human rights was a political
asset for Carter during the 1976 campaign, it became a
political necessity for him in the White House. He had to
be quick and forthright to establish his credentials on the
issue. Both the public and Congress were watching for
followthrough on the campaign promises, and events
also forced the president's hand, long before his administration had sorted out what it should do about human
rights. Most senior officials within the administration

later stressed that Carter had little choice but to respond promptly and publicly. For one, Andrei Sakharov, the Soviet nuclear physicist and dissident leader, wrote a letter which reached the White House just eight days after Carter's 1977 inaugural. It was hard, if not impossible politically, for him to ignore after making such an issue during the 1976 campaign of Gerald Ford's refusal to meet with exiled Soviet author, Alexandr Solzhenitsyn. Later in his presidency, Carter risked criticism for what some journalists labelled a "retreat on human rights" when he responded to criticism of his so-called "open-mouth diplomacy" with more recourse to efforts behind the scenes.

Developments within the Congress also contributed to increased focus on human rights. Stress on human rights, with its appeal to both conservatives and liberals, cut conveniently across the spectrum of congressional concerns. Human rights was thus one of the few issues that could make Jesse Helms, conservative Republican from North Carolina, and James Abourezk, leftwing maverick from South Dakota, vote alike. There was no such thing as a pure vote on human rights.

Those who rallied around the 1977 human-rights amendment regarding the participation of the United States in the IFI's included liberals, dedicated to promotion of human rights; conservatives who opposed any form of foreign aid; those worried about the administration's requests for flexibility; some also wanted to catch Carter on his own campaign rhetoric. A few Democrats supported the amendment, but mainly because they represented districts where organized labor was strong and critical of foreign aid that fostered low-wage imports. Congressmen, who had not given the issue much thought at all (from the south and southwest) were willing to trade support for human rights for protection against imports of palm oil, sugar, or citrus fruit. It was that last group of supporters for tacking human rights criteria onto U.S. votes in the multilateral banks that Senator Daniel P. Moynihan (Democrat of New York) opposed. Distressed by language linking American concern for freedom with that for sugar cane, he said, with palpable disdain and no little Irish oratorical flourish:

> This speaks to the appearance of the integrity of our commitment. How can we stand and ask the rest of the world to follow our example in the field of human rights, and diminish that concern with a proposition having to do with commerce of the most ordinary and everyday type? I ask . . . how would it have been thought if the signers of the Declaration of Independence had concluded that immortal document by stating, 'We mutually pledge to each other our lives, our fortunes and our sacred honor, and further promise to increase the tariffs on soybeans'?[14]

Several other developments brought about increased support for human rights. There was, for example, what amounted to a revolution on Capitol Hill itself. That is, more than half of the national legislators have come to Washington since 1974. Most new members, molded by reaction against the Vietnam War, believe that they can do as well, if not better, than the executive branch on foreign policy. More members of the Congress are interested in foreign policy because of their growing appreciation for the impact of international events on their constituents or because of their travels and experiences. Thus, those behind the explosion of foreign policy amendments on the House and Senate floor, need not—and often are not—on the congressional committees traditionally charged with foreign affairs. Nor are all in the Senate. The House, once considered the junior partner in foreign policy, has become increasingly outspoken.

Many of the new members of the Congress are strong individuals with loose party ties and little personal loyalty to the president. Many exhibit pronounced skepticism about traditional political institutions and toward those who advocate a "responsible" approach to foreign policy, that is, submitting to bipartisanship and seniority. Many got to Washington by running against it. Stress on human rights is thus a natural issue for these new legislators.

Those members who stress human rights want to be effective. During the last decade, many have become convinced that words, while important, cannot accomplish much. Repressive regimes can ignore denunciations in the United Nations. They have more trouble ignoring the delay or rejection of a loan request—or threat of same. Such action can force them to reorder their own programs and, often, suffer other setbacks. Rejection of a major loan request by the World Bank can scare off new private investment. There is thus a tendency to make most initiatives on human rights revolve around efforts to cut off official aid and thereby dissociate the United States from dictators. More recent Congressional actions on human rights blur distinctions between either aid and trade or operations in the public and private sectors.

Advocacy of human rights has the apparent added allure of having few costs. For example, at first blush, it satisfies fiscal conservatives because the initiatives on human rights seem to require little money. And Congress can milk the human rights issue, undaunted by its own often inconsistent approaches to the question. The political dynamics behind the advocacy of human rights

by Americans are such that there need be no close correlation between the barbarity of violations abroad and the
intensity of congressional response. The greatest push
for international protest usually reflects the strongest
domestic political pressure.

Therein lies the special role of the human-rights
lobby. Its work has often been a decisive factor propelling recent promotion of human rights by the United
States. That lobby is concentrated on Capitol Hill in
Washington and near the United Nations in New York,
but backed up by extensive national and international
networks. It has grown dramatially since the early 1970s,
from a relative handful of groups that had little voice, to
over 50 organizations that can and do exercise considerable clout. They achieve much of their impact through
providing testimony before the Congress and background information for its legislation, as well as testimony and information for U.N. deliberations, pressure
on multinational firms, and extensive mailings and educational efforts.

The human-rights lobby has often been able to wield
influence disproportionate to its numbers because of its
sophisticated appeal to diverse interests on Capitol Hill.
It has attracted some supporters for human rights restrictions because some congressmen are genuinely
interested in promoting human rights and think that
such restrictions are the most effective means to that
end. It has gained backing from conservatives who welcome any excuse to cut foreign aid. It has appealed to
the political egos of other legislators who resent programs, such as those for the international financial institutions, that escape direct Congressional control. Henry
Reuss, Chairman of the House Banking Committee,
acknowledged the importance of this lobby in 1978
when he said that he accepted a strong human rights

amendment on a bill to contribute $1.7 billion to a special loan program of the International Monetary Fund because "we need the votes of Mr. Harkin and his dogged band of human righters."[15]

Advocates of human rights, face some obstacles. There are, in addition to numerous international factors, several significant domestic political variables that inhibit stress on human rights. First, promotion of human rights raises difficult issues of implementation for the president which may, in turn, affect the political fortunes of the White House. Whether emphasis on human rights turns from a political asset to a liability depends on how effectively the Chief Executive manages the potential contradictions of a foreign policy that stresses promotion of human rights in the face of domestic interests. Thus, President Carter found early that politics requires compromise and leaves little room for moral purity. His administration, for example, had to approve the request of Congressman Charles Wilson (Democrat of Texas), a close friend of Nicaraguan President Somoza, for assistance to Nicaragua in 1978, despite that government's poor performance on human rights, so that Wilson would support the administration's package on foreign aid.

Carter also found, as any president would, that it is hard to institutionalize official stress on human rights. With or without a president committed to making human rights a major factor in American foreign policy, the idea of human rights is sufficiently controversial and complex to invite substantial opposition. Part of the resistance is due to some bureaucratic politics, but some also is the result of an honest difference of opinion within the executive branch. For example, in 1978, the departments of State and Commerce were strongly opposed to the decision, taken by President Carter and favored by Brzezinski and Secretary of Energy James Schlesinger, to place all exports of technology to the Soviet Union under government control and thus express displeasure with the Soviets' sentencing of the dissident Shcharansky. Predictably, Pentagon officials put more emphasis on the balance of power and their counterparts at Treasury and Commerce put more stress on the balance of payments and trade, than on promotion of human rights.

Second, promotion of human rights carries some risk for the Congress. The fact that the issue prospered politically during much of the 1970s, by means of an often extraordinary alliance of diverse interests, betrays its coincident strength—and weakness. The issue can, as suggested by the vote on human-rights criteria for decisions made in the United States in multilateral banks, be all things to all members. It can also be vulnerable to a splintering of support. For example, blacks in the House of Representatives often resent those congressmen who advocate human rights abroad, at the apparent expense of blacks and Hispanics in the United States. They also clash with colleagues who are reluctant to impose economic sanctions against South African apartheid.

Third, there are limits to public support from Americans for human rights. Attention to human rights is ultimately a creature of constituency appeal. Voters can turn against those who support a policy they perceive as contrary to their other interests. Played out according to one logical conclusion of statements made by members of both the Congress and the executive branch, stress on human rights could cost more, in terms of lost trade and allies, than most Americans want to pay. Played out according to a more limited scenario, it could be impaled on its own raised expectations. Sole reliance on quiet diplomacy in a few inconspicuous quarters will not have dramatic impact. Most Americans like prompt and positive results from their foreign policy. Since promotion of human rights must be a part of a long-term process, stress on the issue can foster short-term frustration within the public and thus negative repercussions for some politicians. Like *détente,* as espoused by Henry Kissinger, the issue of human rights runs the risk of being oversold and promising too much too fast. Should such disillusionment set in, Congress would be inclined to put some brakes on the human rights movement. With the defeat in the 1978 congressional elections of Senator Dick Clark (Democrat of Iowa) and Representative Fraser, there are fewer well-known advocates of human rights to support human rights.

Most Americans favor quiet diplomacy over speaking out vigorously. A strong majority opts for a selective, case-by-case policy that denies benefits only where such actions get desired results and do not hurt other American interests. Thus, concerning human rights in the Soviet Union, the dominant and consistent view has been to accord promotion of human rights second place behind stopping the arms race and preventing war. Fewer than 10 percent urge top priority for human rights.

Further, although the human-rights movement of the 1970s derived much of its impetus from the civil rights campaign in the 1960s, there is another aspect to the connection. Many whites a decade ago were all for equality of racial opportunity until a black moved next door. Similarly, many Americans today are all for proclamations on behalf of international human rights, but against increasing their taxes to pay for more foreign aid. The citizens' support for human rights is, in short, more complex than it may appear. As with the often unholy congressional alliance for human rights, the human rights public consists of many parts. Its very diversity may make solidarity more apparent than real.

SOME CONCLUSIONS

Several conclusions emerge from the preceding discussion. First, the issue is affected by a struggle between the legislative and executive branches of the government, views of various interest groups, and American public opinion. Domestic political considerations shape both the general direction and specific focus of American foreign policy on human rights: What are the main targets of this concern? What tools will be used? There is no consistent relationship between the extent of the violation of human rights abroad and the strength of the reaction of the United States to the violation. Thus, the coincidence, in the 1970s, of a general disregard by Americans for massive genocide in Cambodia but concentration on relatively few Jewish dissidents in the Soviet Union. No victim of violations can assume that the delicate balance between domestic political needs of the United States and action by Americans on human rights abroad will tip in his favor. Several congressmen have admitted that legislative restrictions against countries violating human rights may result from the fact that pressure is applied to Congress rather than from the awareness of the relative brutality of repression in other nations.

Second, much of the course of diplomacy towards human rights by the United States is predictable precisely because of the domestic determinants behind the policy. The key indices lie in public opinion polls, the composition of the Congress, and the incumbent of the White House. The key questions revolve around who stands to gain by promotion of human rights, where, and how.

Third, American political history reveals that the nation's record is mixed. There has been substantial American sacrifice to make the world a better and freer place. There has also, sometimes, been a self-serving tendency to save American souls first and worry about the consequences later. Critics are not all wrong when they condemn some promotion of human rights by the United States as a domestic political gimmick. The United States is much like other nations. Its performance suggests that it has no unique claim on mission or morality. If there is to be longer-term credibility for American policy on human rights, national myth might, most usefully, catch up with that reality.

Further, making human rights a source or surrogate for domestic consensus behind American foreign policy has been, and remains, an exercise in wish fulfillment. Since 1789, the support of human rights by the United States has been affected by contradictory impulses at home from differing ethnic and regional groups, economic interests, political parties, and ambitious individuals. Representatives from each group have, on different occasions, led the nation in diametrically opposed directions. During the earliest years of the Republic, leaders, such as George Washington and John Quincy Adams, did not support the cause of human rights. They followed this policy because they realized that the United States could not intervene effectively on behalf of oppressed people abroad. Dwight Eisenhower did not adhere to the policy either, and for the same reason, when the Soviet Union intervened in Hungary in 1956. Woodrow Wilson, in contrast, tried but failed, with the Fourteen Points, to make more Americans support institutions that might serve human rights and the national interest as well. Then, as more recently, Americans got the human rights policy they thought they wanted and were willing to pay for.

Troubling as some U.S. reaction may be, there has been a shift in the last half of the twentieth century toward a more sophisticated public perception of America's role in the world and the relation of human rights to other objectives of the United States. The contrast between resistance to the Treaty of Versailles and "return to normalcy" in the 1920s and American leadership 20 years later in the United Nations, the Marshall Plan, and Truman Doctrine is instructive.

At the same time, that shift has created some unexpected problems of its own. Cash for containment of communism had domestic support and diplomatic effect particularly pertinent to the immediate postwar period. However, cultivation of anticommunist allies in the 1950s came to haunt the United States by the 1970s. Nations like South Korea drew belated fire for violations of human rights, often as serious as those which had caused early condemnation of communist governments. Viewed from the perspective of concern for human rights, the fervent anticommunism of the fifties became a partial embarrassment during the seventies, with parts of the executive branch scrambling to redress the alleged imbalance in national security seen by parts of the American public and Congress.

If the past gives pause to complacent invocation of the American Dream, so does the future. Predictions about the coming course of the emphasis that the United States will place on human rights range between two extremes. Critics of an activist policy claim that stress on human rights will disappear, little-mourned. Proponents see a prohuman rights policy as the cutting edge of a new definition of national interest.

The likely outcome, as with so much else in American politics, is a little of both. Other issues will no doubt replace human rights in press headlines. Indeed, they already have. Support of fundamental freedoms is, however, not likely to fade away completely, Violations of human rights will continue to impinge on American concerns, be they strictly humanitarian or expressly self-ish. If ignored, they will mock Americans' view, however idealized, of themselves. And, they will undermine American political and economic interests. Stress on human rights, for those reasons and others, has a certain self-propulsion. It takes much time and effort to undo legislation in the United States on the subject. According to Congressman Harkin, "We have established a body of law that will be hard to reverse; precedents are set for the State Department and others." It takes even more time to dismantle international machinery. In addition, those who advocated political participation, justice, equal opportunity, and free expression in the 1960s continue to view themselves as a political vanguard. But with the mission now to rethink old conceptions about national priorities and to promote human rights. And, it is more difficult still to reverse the flow of world public opinion. In the unlikely event that Americans were to forget about the issue, there are others elsewhere who are forcing their political leaders to pay more attention to human rights. For example, in Canada, large communities of refugees from Eastern Europe and Latin America hold their parliamentarians accountable on this issue. There is growing attention, promoted by major human rights organizations in the United States, to efforts like the transfer amendments offered in 1978 by Representative Parren Mitchell and Senator George McGovern. They recommended shifting funds within the federal budget from "wasteful and dangerous military programs" to stress on housing, nutrition, and health care. They are asking for what amounts to a significant shift in American perspectives and priorities. To a large degree, their efforts reflect objectives set forth in the U.N. Universal Declaration of Human Rights, particularly those portions devoted to fulfilling economic and social rights.

Efforts to realize the rights contained in the Universal Declaration could well require a considerable redistribution of income within the United States and further adjustment in the relationship between government and private enterprise. The economic dimension of American human rights diplomacy may depend on the political will of the bottom billion of the world's poor—and what connection American policy-makers make between the two. The recurrent conservatism of most Americans and the nation's current political mood suggest that, for the foreseeable future, most Americans will balk at the great cost to themselves of principle. Most politicians will take their cue on human rights accordingly.

Considerable as the cost for an effective American policy on human rights may be, however, there is some reason to believe that there may, over time, be some shift in domestic sentiment. President Carter has asserted that Americans cannot denounce others abroad without improving their own performance on human rights. Spokesmen for other nations are quick to argue that credibility for American policy on human righs rests on precisely that point. Public opinion polls taken in the United States confirm a related point: Most Americans feel most strongly, when asked about human rights, that "we should set a good example protecting and enlarging human rights here at home."

Much of the ultimate significance of American policy on human rights may lie in such domestic impact. The effect could range from closing political and economic gaps for women, blacks, and Hispanics in the United States, to assuring dignity for the elderly and providing reasonably priced health care for all Americans. Eventually, more vocal and better organized minorities may challenge the majority in the United States. And, for its part, the majority itself may find promotion of human rights, at home and abroad, is to its longer-term interest.

NOTES

1. Some material in this discussion is adapted from the second chapter of my book, *What Price Principle?—U.S. Policy on Human Rights.*
2. For a more extensive discussion of the *foreign* politics of human rights, see Sandra Vogelgesang, "What Price Principle? U.S. Policy on Human Rights," *Foreign Affairs,* Vol. 56, No. 4 (July 1978), pp. 819-841.
3. For more discussion on the general subject of foreign policy and the democratic process and the specific shifts relations between Congress and the executive branch, see the articles by James Chace, Lee H. Hamilton and Michael H. Van Dusen, and Douglas J. Bennet, Jr., *Foreign Affairs,* Vol. 57, No. 1 (Fall, 1978), pp. 1-50.
4. For other speeches of particular note, see "The Moral Foundations of Foreign Policy," Minneapolis, July 15, 1975; his address before the Synagogue Council of America, New York, October 19, 1976; and his speech before the New York University Graduate School of Business Administration, New York, September 19, 1977.
5. "Human Rights in the World Community: a Call for U.S. Leadership," Report of the Subcommittee on International Organizations and Movements of the Committee on Foreign Affairs, House of Representatives, March 27, 1974, p. 9.

6. See the exchange of correspondence in the appendix of published hearings, "International Protection of Human Rights, the Work of International Organizations and the Role of U.S. Foreign Policy," August 1-December 7, 1973, House Subcommittee on International Organizations and Movements, pp. 804-873.
7. For a list of those hearings, see material provided at the end of this chapter.
8. These letters are included in the series, *Digest of the United States Practice in International Law, 1974,* Department of State Publication 8809, pp. 145-153. The *Digest*, published annually, provides a superbly comprehensive summary of recent actions and statements made by the Congress and the executive branch on human rights.
9. For a more extensive discussion of the "Economics of Human Rights," see Chapter Three of my book, cited in footnote 1.
10. Senator Alan Cranston (Democrat of California) sent a particularly sharply worded letter to Secretary Kissinger, November 5, 1975.
11. Department of State, "Report to the Congress on the Human Rights Situation in Countries Receiving U.S. Security Assistance," November 14, 1975.
12. From the statement made on the Senate floor by Senator Cranston, November 20, 1975.
13. Quoted in the *New York Times* (September 9, 1976).
14. Quoted by David S. Broder, "Palm Oil, Citrus, Sugar Cane—and Human Rights?" *Washington Post* (July 24, 1977).
15. Quoted in the *Washington Post* (February 24, 1978).

CONGRESSIONAL HEARINGS AND DOCUMENTS ON HUMAN RIGHTS

Human Rights in the World Community: A Call for U.S. Leadership. March 27, 1974. (Report of the Subcommittee on International Organizations and Movements—hereafter referred to as IO)

International Protection of Human Rights: the Work of International Organizations and the Role of U.S. Foreign Policy. August 1; September 13, 19, 20, 27; October 3, 4, 10, 11, 16, 18, 24, 25; November 1; December 7, 1973. Before IO.

Human Rights in Chile (Part I). December 9, 1973; May 7, 23; June 11, 12, and 18, 1974. Before IO and the Subcommittee on Inter-American Affairs.

Treatment of Israeli POW's in Syria and Their Status under the Geneva Convention. February 26, 1974. Before IO.

Problems of Protecting Civilians Under International Law in the Middle East Conflict. April 4, 1974. Before IO.

Human Righs in Africa: Report by the International Commission on Jurists. June 13, 1974. Before IO.

Review of the U.N. Commission on Human Rights. June 18 and 20, 1974. Before IO.

Soviet Union: Human Rights and Detente. July 17 and 25, 1974. Before IO and Subcommittee on Europe.

Torture and Oppression in Brazil. December 11, 1974. Before IO.

Human Rights in South Korea and the Philippines: Implications for U.S. Policy. May 20, 22; June 3, 5, 10, 12, 17, 24, 1975. Before IO.

Human Rights in Chile (Part 2). November 19, 1974. Before IO and Subcommittee on Inter-American Affairs.

Human Rights in South Korea: Implications for U.S. Policy. July 31, August 5, December 20, 1974. Before IO and Subcommittee on Asian and Pacific Affairs.

Human Rights in Haiti. November 18, 1975. Before IO.

Human Rights In Chile. December 9, 1975. Before IO.

Chile: The Status of Human Rights and Its Relationship to U.S. Economic Assistance Programs. April 29; May 5, 1976. Before IO.

Psychiatric Abuse of Political Prisoners in the Soviet Union: Testimony by Leonid Plyushch. March 30, 1976. Before IO.

Human Rights in Indonesia and the Philippines. December 18 and May 3, 1976. Before IO.

Anti-Semitism and Reprisals Against Jewish Emigration in the Soviet Union. May 27, 1976. Before IO.

Human Rights in the Philippines: Report by Amnesty International. September 15, 1976. Before IO.

Human Rights Issues at the Sixth Regular Session of the Organization of American States General Assembly. August 10, 1976. Before IO.

Religious Persecution in the Soviet Union. June 24 and 30, 1976. Before IO and Subcommittee on International Political and Military Affairs.

Human Rights in Iran. August 3 and September 8, 1976. Before IO.

Human Rights in Nicaragua, Guatemala, and El Salvador. June 8 and 9, 1976. Before IO.

Human Rights in India. June 23, 28, and 29, and September 16 and 23, 1976. Before IO.

Human Rights in Uruguay and Paraguay. June 17; July 27, 28; and August 4, 1976. Before IO.

Namibia: The United Nations and U.S. Policy. August 24 and 27, 1976. Before IO.

Human Rights in Argentina. September 28 and 29, 1976. Before IO.

Human Rights in North Korea. September 9, 1976. Before IO.

The Recent Presidential Elections in El Salvador: Implications for U.S. Foreign Policy. March 9 and 17, 1977. Before IO and Subcommittee on Inter-American Affairs.

Human Rights in East Timor and the Question of the Use of U.S. Equipment by the Indonesian Armed Forces. March 23, 1977. Before IO and Subcommittee on Asian and Pacific Affairs.

Human Rights Practices in Countries Receiving U.S. Security Assistance. Report Submitted to the House Committee on International Relations by the Department of State. April 25, 1977.

Human Rights in Cambodia. May 3, 1977. Before IO.

Review of the United Nations Thirty-third Commission on Human Rights. May 19, 1977. Before IO.

Human Rights in Taiwan. June 14, 1977. Before IO.

Human Rights in East Timor. June 28 and July 19, 1977. Before IO.

Human Rights in the International Community and in U.S. Foreign Policy, 1945-76. July 24, 1977. Report of the Subcommittee on International Organizations.

The Status of Human Rights in Selected Countries and the U.S. Response. July 25, 1977. Report of the Subcommittee on International Organizations.

Human Rights in Cambodia. July 26, 1977. Before IO.

Human Rights Issues at the Seventh Regular Session of the Organization of American States General Assembly. September 15, 1977. Before IO.

Human Rights In Indonesia: A Review of the Situation with Respect to the Long-term Political Detainees. October 18, 1977. Before IO.

Human Rights in Iran. October 26, 1977. Before IO.

Country Reports on Human Rights Practices. February 3, 1978. Report Submitted to the Committee on International Relations of the U.S. House of Representatives and Committee on Foreign Relations of the U.S. Senate by the Department of State.

Human Rights in the Philippines: Recent Developments. April 27, 1978. Before IO.

Human Rights Conditions in Selected Countries and the U.S. Response. July 25, 1978. Prepared for IO by the Library of Congress.

Human Rights and the Foreign Policy of the United States: South Africa

JOHN DE ST. JORRE

The Republic of South Africa is a country which combines an odious policy towards human rights with an array of strategic and economic resources. This presents the West with the dilemma of balancing moral distaste against material need.

South Africa's qualifications as a delinquent in the field of human rights are impeccable. The white minority, about 17 percent of the total population, govern the unrepresented nonwhite majority. The whites also have allotted 87 percent of the country to themselves, and in that area the nonwhites have no political rights. Since the accession of the ruling National party to power in 1948, the irreversibility of this dispensation has been made an act of faith of the government, of the party and, by and large, of the Afrikaner people who constitute 60 percent of the white population and who have developed a cohesive and robust nationalism of their own. During that period, the separation of the races has been codified and refined. The coloreds (mixed) and the "browns" were disenfranchised from the white parliament where they used to be represented. Also "black spots" of settlement in white zones were removed. Later, under pressure from abroad, alternatives were offered to the disenfranchised and dispossessed to soften the *baaskap*, or white supremacist, image of the government.

Under the guidance of Dr. Hendrik Vervoerd in the late fifties and early sixties, the Bantustan plan was proposed, and South Africa's nine major African tribes were encouraged, first, to seek self-government and later, independence. (The bulk of the natural and manmade riches of South Africa remain in white hands.) The Transkei, the biggest of the Bantustans, and Bophuthatswana have become independent and many of the other smaller and fragmented homelands are expected to follow suit. About half the black population of 18 million lives in the homelands under the rule of traditional chiefs, enjoying some political and civil rights not available in the republic but lacking the economic opportunities across the border. The rest of the blacks are designated as "foreign workers," although most of them were neither born in their "homeland" nor have any wish to go there. Their rights in white South Africa, the land of their birth, are those of the migrant laborer, a black *gasterbeiter* who is allowed to live temporarily in a township or farm, sell his labor to the whites, obey the laws of the country, and, when he is no longer needed, pack his bag and go "home." The other racial groups, the coloreds and Indians, were not allotted homelands but have been given their own elected bodies whose leaders meet with the white government at cabinet level. They actually have little real power in shaping the laws and ordering the priorities that govern their lives.

The South African government's rhetoric in recent years emphasizes the difficulty of disparate ethnic groups living together. In a unitary system of government, the South Africans point to the inevitability of conflict, of one group trying to dominate another. They cite current examples: Cyprus, Lebanon, Ulster. They see the trend of mini-nationalism growing fast and refer to the Scots, to the Bengalis, and to the Quebecois. Closer to home, they stress the cultural and economic gaps between the whites of South Africa and the other races and to the animosities that divide tribes in Africa. They reject majority, that is, black rule. They look at Africa and say where does the majority rule in that huge continent? In Western democratic terms, they have a point. Most African states, although they may be ruled in the general interest of the majority, do not technically enjoy majority rule. Minority rule prevails farther afield, in the communist countries and in much of the third world. In short, political rights are a rare commodity, so why pick on South Africa all the time?

The answer is twofold. First, if South Africa were to show a genuine and sustained concern with finding a more equitable system to sharing power with its non-white majority, it would undoubtedly receive a more sympathetic hearing abroad. A minority of its whites, both English and Afrikaners, feel passionately that there is a middle way between exclusive white and exclusive black rule. Many blacks also believe this, and a search for a middle path has begun. But the Nationalist government only recognizes two stark alternatives: white salvation through apartheid and white perdition through its abandonment. Second, although ethnic incompatabilities are a reality, and it would be foolish not to take them into account in structuring any society, there is no doubt that discrimination in South Africa has always been, and remains, racial. The government implies that this is not so, that "differentiation"—the new vogue word for apartheid—is simply the best way for ethnic groups to keep their distance and avoid conflict. But all whites—Afrikaners, English, newly arrived German and Italian immigrants, and so on—are treated one way, and all blacks—Zulus, Tswanas, Xhosas—are treated another.

The color of the skin you were born with, and have no power to choose or change, is the central determinant of your existence; the lives, say, of a black doctor, a Portuguese illiterate, or a colored plumber will be conditioned primarily not by their respective skills but by that immutable and highly visible pigmentation.

If that were all, South Africa might not be cast among the worst of the pariahs. After all, many countries deny their citizens political rights and many governments and individuals are guilty of racial discrimination. But there are two additional factors that have to be considered. The first concerns the totality of discrimination and the consequent loss of rights—all rights, political, social, economic, civic and so on—for blacks. South Africa is unique in the way that its government has institutionalized racial discrimination by countless statutes, laws, administrative directives, education, and by daily practice.

The racial character of South Africa, which permeates every aspect of its life, also stands out because of the double standard inherent in the political system. A minority governs democratically. It has a Westminster-style parliament and cabinet. There are elections at regular intervals, free debate, and a relatively free press. However, blacks have no part in this political process. Whites are legally permitted to bargain collectively; blacks are not. Whites have compulsory and free education; blacks do not. Whites can move freely about the country, and work and settle where they wish; blacks cannot. Whites may acquire any skill they are capable of mastering and do business where they wish; blacks may not.

Perhaps one of the most iniquitous, and least publicized, facets of the apartheid system is the carefully structured education of the children of South Africa. The blacks are given "Bantu education" stressing the importance of tribal languages, customs, and ethnic differences—something the rest of Africa is trying to avoid. The whites are provided a "European education" highlighting their non-African heritage and feeding them stereotypes of their superiority, as human beings and rulers, to the nonwhites. Grade six geography books in white South African schools categorize Europeans as those people who fill all the professional jobs. Indians work as traders, and coloreds are employed as carpenters, masons, among other trades; the Bantu work as servants, laborers, and garden boys.

Any move by the majority to change the system, no matter how peacefully it may be conducted, is brusquely suppressed by the government. The government will jail anyone who tries to bring about change for indefinite periods of time without charge or trial, and prisoners, especially political prisoners, are tortured regularly. Forty detainees have died mysteriously in jail during the last decade. The authorities say these, and many more who suffered a similar fate, committed suicide. Some probably did when death became preferable to life in the cells; but medical and other evidence also suggests brutal treatment and, in effect, murder by the state. The South African government has also devised a method of silencing individuals outside its prisons. Political activists can be confined to their homes for lengthy periods of time and denied the right to meet more than one person at a time; Their writings and publications also can be banned.

After the Nationalist party came to power in 1948, four broad phases in United States-South African relations can be discerned. During the fifties, Washington looked upon South Africa with a detached benevolence, helped no doubt by the recent memories of their brotherhood-in-arms in the Second World War and in

Korea. Links between the navies of the two countries remained strong but Africa, in general, was still regarded as the domain of the European colonial powers. The early sixties witnessed dramatic changes on the continent and a shift in American perceptions. Many African colonies threw off their colonial status and became members of the United Nations; South Africa left the British Commonwealth and became a republic with a penchant for isolation. The United States, under Kennedy, shifted its policies in favor of the black nations. This policy was continued by Johnson but was reversed under Nixon when the NSSM 39 review was written under the direction of Henry Kissinger in 1969. NSSM 39 changed the policy of the United States back in favor of the white regimes of southern Africa. The new policy was maintained after Nixon's administration, but Kissinger, shocked by the Angolan experience, then became somewhat more sympathetic towards the Africans during his visits to the continent in 1976 and his attempt to defuse the Rhodesian crisis. President Carter's administration has accelerated the rapprochement with black Africa and adopted a cool attitude toward South Africa.

American interest in the Republic of South Africa has traditionally focused on four areas: the country's strategic location on the Cape route; its treasure trove of minerals, especially those used in space and armament programs; its profitable market for exports and investment from the United States; and its contribution to the stability of the region. Ever since the United States began to evolve an African policy in the early sixties, the policy to be adopted to deal with these considerations has been the subject of a continuous, often heated, but inconclusive debate. The controversy remained inconclusive, however, because there was no question of American interests being seriously threatened at that time. During the sixties and early seventies when other parts of Africa were in turmoil, southern Africa was stable. It was only when a fresh surge of African nationalism, accompanied by an unprecedented degree of Soviet and Cuban involvement, disturbed the tranquility of the region that United States policy-makers began to take a new look at both their interests in the area and the best way to protect them.

South Africa, in the early sixties, provided a rare example of Washington showing sensitivity to the human rights issue and allowing it to influence the direction of policy. The Kennedy Administration decided to court the newly independent states in the black north and to distance itself from the governments of the white south. In 1963, it imposed an arms embargo on the Republic of South Africa, the first Western power to do so and shortly before the United Nations endorsed a similar sanction. However, there really was little danger of south Africa voluntarily offering its strategic valuables to a hostile power. Nor was there much danger that the South African government would be deprived of them by force because the country was protected by a buffer zone of white-controlled allies and was growing stronger, economically and militarily, each year.

Third-world countries usually have the option of bartering their resources with the West or the East; they also tend to be frail politically and militarily. The big powers find themselves in competition in places such as Zaire, then the Congo in the early sixties, for example. And the small countries sometimes try to exploit that rivalry, not always successfully but with a certain freedom of choice. South Africa, because of its historical Western orientation and its poor reputation among third-world and communist nations, is denied that choice.

After Britain's arms embargo in 1964, France, Italy, Belgium, and other countries continued to supply the republic with the military hardware it required to sustain the strength and stability on which Western interests were deemed to depend. Direct American involvement in South Africa in the sixties was small because Washington's foreign policy priorities were elsewhere, in places like Vietnam and the Middle East. Cynics point out that Kennedy's administration could easily afford a liberal pro-black policy in Africa because little was at stake and, what there was, came conveniently under the protection of good friends and allies. The cynics were, I think, partly correct although it would be wrong to impugn the strong humanitarian principles of many members of the Kennedy and Johnson administrations and their success in defending their position against those in the government who urged a friendlier policy towards Pretoria.

A third factor in assessing the role of human rights as a motivating principle in the American tilt against South Africa was domestic opinion. For a multi-ethnic nation with a sizeable black population, race is bound to be an issue. In the early sixties, it could perhaps be said it was the issue, eclipsed only by the Vietnam War in the later years of the decade. As the United States became more conscious of its own racial problems, it was inevitable that it should show greater sensitivity towards other racially troubled countries. There was a number of special interest lobbies—churches, radical groups, civil rights movements and so on—concerned about American policy. It was the time of liberation, of a new interest in personal freedoms; it was the time also perhaps when racial guilt began to stir and people sought ways to make amends. The groups that were advocating human rights were opposed by some conservatives, and military men who believed, as Kissinger and Nixon later did, that the white status quo in southern Africa was not going to be disturbed and that the best way to protect American interests was to recognize that fact and work with those governments. But the liberals kept the upper hand although it is interesting to note that it was only in 1967, four years after the arms embargo had been imposed, that the United States Navy stopped paying goodwill visits to South African ports, finally rejecting the principle of separate entertainment facilities ashore for black and white seamen.

With the demise of the Democratic administration, however, United States policy changed. In 1969, Henry Kissinger became Nixon's national security adviser and ordered a review of American options in Africa. This was the time when the white regimes on the continent looked secure and virtually impregnable. Rhodesia had broken away from Britain four years earlier and, despite United Nations sanctions which the United States had supported, showed no signs of weakening. The wars in the Portuguese territories dragged on, draining Portugal of its meager treasure, but without having any discernible effect on the policy-makers in Lisbon where Caetano had taken over from the moribund Salazar. South Africa was enjoying a period of unprecedented peace and prosperity.

National Security Study Memorandum 39, which resulted from Kissinger's reappraisal of American interests and options in southern Africa, makes fascinating reading. It was probably the first coherent attempt by government to describe all the interests that connected the United States with Africa and to put the whole into a proper perspective. Input for the study came from the Departments of State, Defense and Commerce, the Treasury, the Joint Chiefs of Staff and the CIA. The document refrained from advocating a particular policy line; rather, it confirmed the view of previous administrations that American interests in Africa, though economically and politically important, were not vital to the security of the United States and that the continent was not of major importance. It then spelled out the nature of the objectives.

1. To improve the standing of the United States in black Africa and internationally on the race issue.

2. To minimize the likelihood of escalation of violence in the area and risk of any involvement by the United States.

3. To minimize the opportunities for the Soviet Union and Communist China to exploit the racial issue in the region for propaganda advantage and to gain political influence with black governments and liberation movements.

4. To encourage moderation of the current rigid racial and colonial policies of the white regimes.

5. To protect economic, scientific, and strategic interests and opportunities in the region, including the orderly marketing of South Africa's gold production.

It was acknowledged that some of these aims were conflicting and irreconcilable. The options, as opposed to the objectives, fell into two basic categories. Options 1, 4, and 5 advised strong support for one party or another or total disengagement: "all or nothing" options, as it were. Options 2 and 3 were more circumspect, the former suggested that the United States should support white governments on the premise that "the whites are here to stay and the only way that constructive change can come about is through them"; the latter advocated a continuation of the policy Kennedy and Johnson had followed of limiting association with the white states on the understanding that "the situation in the region is not likely to change appreciably in the foreseeable future, and in any event we cannot influence it." The State Department later denied that Option 2 was adopted as official policy and, technically, that is true. However, a significant number of the "operational examples" (measures that could be used to implement a policy option) listed under Option 2 became realities during the Nixon-Ford years, too many for it to be regarded as pure coincidence. However, because of the shift in the balance of power in southern Africa the premises of Options 2 and 3 are no longer valid. The whites may not be "here to stay" for much longer; they have already quit Angola and Mozambique and their future is uncertain in Rhodesia and Namibia. The situation in the region is, in fact, changing every day. Although NSSM 39 was written in 1969 and although Kissinger is no longer in office, the divisions that the study revealed in the policy-making process still exist. The Africa Bureau in the State Department retains its liberal image which, admittedly, now looks less exciting today than it did when it was battling against the conservatism of a Republican administration. Defense, Commerce, the Treasury, and the CIA seem to be more confused than they used to be about how the South African issue should be tackled although the Navy still thinks friendly cooperation with Pretoria is the best way of safeguarding America's strategic interests. NSSM 39 also noted the congressional lobby groups, the black caucus versus the southern conservatives, and there is no reason to suppose that they are any less important today than they were a decade ago. Indeed, the Angolan civil war and the significance now attached to crucial natural resources has awakened a new strategic interest in Africa, animated the debate and increased the influence of the special interest groups.

NSSM 39 was revealing in that none of the policy options mentioned human rights. They only talked of the "racial issue" or "discrimination," of the desirability of "progress" for the blacks, of "participation" in a white power structure, and so on. Neither did the document refer to the Africans' desire for majority rule. The racial stigmata of South Africa was stressed and it was accepted that "the racial or colonial policies of the white regimes" could not be endorsed. But there was no suggestion that concern for the racial issue sprang from any other source than the pragmatic one that South Africa's policies had made it a target for international hostility and that was a fact of life which had to be recognized. In discussing the areas where there was a basic consensus within the United States government, NSSM 39 includes this revealing paragraph.

"Our political interests in the region are important because the racial policies of the white states have become a major international issue. *Therefore, because other countries have made it so, our foreign policy must take into account the domestic policies of the white regimes.* Most non-white nations in the world in varying degrees would tend to judge conspicuous U.S. co-operation with the white regimes as condoning their racial policies [my italics]."

In summary, Kissinger's main interest was entirely pragmatic and short term. The United States had important but not vital interests in South Africa. However, they were not yet directly threatened. Thus the best policy was to support South Africa in a low-keyed manner so that American interests in black Africa would not be jeopardized. Racial and political accommodation in the republic were desirable objectives, but they should be achieved in an evolutionary and peaceful way. And if there was no sign of the government in Pretoria moving in that direction, then there was not much that the

United States or anyone else could do about it. Kissinger later was quoted in the *Washington Post* on September 12, 1973:

> Foreign policy is essentially global strategy . . . and domestic considerations and pressures should not be allowed to impinge on it . . . we have as a country to ask ourselves the question of whether it should be the principal goal of American foreign policy to transform the domestic structure of societies with which we deal or whether the principal exercise of our foreign policy should be toward affecting the foreign policy of those societies.

In the case of South Africa, there was no doubt in his mind that there should be no attempt at domestic transformation; in the case of Chile, he clearly thought otherwise.

After NSSM 39 was written, the United States government became more sympathetic towards the white regimes of southern Africa. The United States delegation in the United Nations began to vote with the British and French to protect the republic, more so than it had done in the past. In 1971, the Byrd Amendment was passed permitting American chrome importers to break Rhodesian sanctions; subsequent attempts to repeal the amendment never received the support of the White House although it was strongly urged by the State Department's Africa Bureau which resented Kissinger's high-handed tactics and was bitter at the backlash his policy had caused among America's black African friends. (The shift also benefited Portugal. Relations with Caetano's government became more friendly and Lisbon received large Export-Import loans in return for allowing the United States to use the Azores base.)

American trade with South Africa was expanded during this period, and investments were increased by 73 percent between 1969 and 1974. The arms embargo was relaxed, and the United States became more closely involved in the republic's nuclear energy program, supplying Pretoria with much of its enriched uranium requirements.

Could it have been otherwise? The combination of Kissinger's global realpolitik, Nixon's conservatism, and strong pressures especially from the large industrialists, the arms manufacturers, and the Pentagon's naval strategists made the shift inevitable. The liberals could not resist, in part because they could not gain popular support for human rights in Africa. Americans were—and are—not very interested in Africa. Historically, there was far less contact with the continent than other third-world areas and, politically, more dramatic things were going on elsewhere, especially in Vietnam. Even American blacks, although becoming increasingly aware of Africa, were too preoccupied in their own struggle for rights at home to have much time or energy left over to support human rights in Africa.

And over everything loomed Vietnam. One third-world imbroglio was enough, particularly an imbroglio of Vietnam's dimensions. A nation, even as large a one as the United States, can be excused perhaps for being none too vigilant about other corners of the world when it has half a million men fighting a war thousands of miles from home in an environment as alien as it is hostile. One can argue that such a calamity might excuse the general public but not the legislators and politicians, whose job it is to monitor their nation's foreign policy. But Congress could not escape the national trauma and nothing that was happening in Africa at that time matched the obsessive quality of the Vietnam War. As it happened, the late sixties and early seventies were relatively stagnant years in Africa, especially in southern Africa. And then Vietnam left its legacy, which is still with us, of disillusionment with foreign involvement and of a powerful disinclination to be trapped into shoring up dubious regimes against international communism in remote and incomprehensible third-world countries.

The Angolan civil war did not throw much light on how the United States problem of conflicting interests in black and white Africa might be resolved, but it did, in a negative sense, perhaps indicate that a new era of foreign policy in which morality could play a part, might be dawning. Kissinger's reaction to Congress cutting off clandestine support to the anti-MPLA forces in Angola was anger, followed later by a reversion to his basic pragmatism. If you can't beat 'em, join 'em, he seemed to say and went to a number of key African capitals, tilting his policy back against the whites, particularly against Ian Smith in Rhodesia. Harsh realities, not human rights, were the main considerations of this new posture. The Portuguese had gone, the Cubans had come, the Rhodesians were doomed, and the Russians were laughing up their sleeves. At the same time, American interests in South Africa looked both more valuable and more vulnerable than they had before the Arab oil boycott and price rise and the Portuguese collapse, the two events that changed America's attitude toward southern Africa in 1973. Kissinger's aim in the region was to defuse the growing conflict and hopefully protect American interests by orchestrating a series of peaceful changes, at least in Rhodesia and Namibia, which would bring black moderate governments to power, thus denying the Soviets and Cubans an opportunity to conduct another "Angola" and giving South Africa more time and more peace on its borders to work out its own salvation. His method was his characteristic arm-twisting step-by-step diplomacy, using South Africa as an additional muscle man. In doing so, he bestowed on Pretoria diplomatic respectability and political kudos, shortlived perhaps but real enough at the time. He achieved partial success with Smith's acceptance of majority rule and then passed into history when Carter beat Ford in the presidential election.

The black upheavals in the republic, as much as the Angolan War, have increased Western interest in the neglected continent. In addition, a shortage of raw materials has increased the attention the West pays to Africa. It possesses rich resources—oil in Nigeria, cobalt in Zaire, copper in Zambia, uranium and diamonds in Namibia, and chrome and gold in South Africa. And suddenly, with Carter, Andrew Young and others, human rights acquired a new importance in the formulation of foreign policy. Even Kissinger, in his last days, began to pay lip service to the concept. In his tough anti-Rhodesian speech in Lusaka in April, 1976, he made a brief reference to South Africa in which he said:

> A peaceful end to institutionalized inequality is in the interest of all South Africa. . . . Our policy toward South Africa is based upon the premise that within a reasonable time we shall see a clear evolution toward equality of opportunity and *basic human rights* (my italics) for all South Africans.

The mood in Congress was also undergoing a transformation. In 1975 it prohibited loans by international institutions to countries that consistently violate human rights. A climate more favorable to human rights had also been created by the Watergate scandal and the congressional investigations of the C.I.A.

In such an atmosphere and with the moral and political weight of President Carter behind it, the Byrd amendment was finally repealed. Washington, in its dealings with Pretoria, made it clear that there would be several departures from the Kissinger policies immediately and that more might follow. First, the United States regarded the Turnhalle exercise in South-West Africa—South Africa's "internal solution" to that territory's problems—as unacceptable. Second, the republic could not expect an easing of pressure over the issue of apartheid as a reward for its cooperation in the search for solutions of the South-West African and Rhodesian crises. And finally, the Carter administration spelled out its view of what the South African government should be aiming at in its own society: full political participation for all races, which meant, in the words of Vice President Walter Mondale, one-man, one-vote, or majority rule.

The coincidence of crisis in southern Africa and an American government committed to human rights presents a challenge and an opportunity to United States foreign policy-makers. Any change in policy requires an analysis of objectives and a fresh look at what is at stake. American interests in South Africa have been radically changed. But now they are threatened by the increasingly volatile situation in southern Africa and, as a result, the alternative methods of protecting them have been brought more sharply into focus. The importance of the republic now lies more so than ever in its strategic geography, its rich and diversified minerals, its value to the American industrialist and businessman, and its capacity for maintaining stability in the region.

The South Africans insist that the country is a vital link in Western defenses and that a white government in Pretoria is the best guardian of that link. The growth of the Soviet fleet in the Indian Ocean and the huge amounts of oil that continue to travel around the Cape to Western Europe and the United States seem to reinforce the South African point of view. Furthermore, ports that used to belong to the NATO alliance under Portuguese control in Angola and Mozambique have been lost to Marxist-oriented black governments, but South Africa still provides the best naval facilities and back-up services in the southern Atlantic. The West, Pretoria argues, should open its eyes and support the most effective bulwark against communism that exists in southern Africa.

There are, however, major flaws—to my mind, conclusive—in this hypothesis. The Western supply line from the oil wells in the Persian Gulf is a long one. If the Soviet Union wished to cut it, there would be many more convenient places to do so than in the southern seas around South Africa. In the current situation, the Soviet Union would know that any interference with such a key route for the West could be construed as an act of war. In a conventional war, the denial of the republic's port facilities by, say, a hostile black government—or worse still, their loss to the Soviet Union—would be serious but by no means fatal to the West's war effort, for the struggle would undoubtedly be decided in areas closer to home than southern Africa. Furthermore, the vulnerability of the crucial oil would continue to be greater at its source, close to the Soviet Union itself, rather than several thousand miles to the south. (A nuclear war would presumably be nasty and short, and principally being conducted in the Northern Hemisphere.)

Perhaps a stronger and more concrete argument against South Africa is that the greatest Soviet threat is not on the water threatening Western lifelines but on the land mass of Africa from the Soviet support of frustrated black nationalism. The Russians have gained much more influence in Africa through backing African nationalist movements against white minority regimes than either through building up their fleet in the Indian Ocean which has resulted in a response by the United States of the development of the base at Diego Garcia, or by trying to lock themselves into defense agreements with people like the Ghanaians, the Egyptians, and the Somalis. In other words, the Russians identified themselves with the forces of African nationalism, supported by the entire third world. The Russians discovered that the West was either complacently neutral or on the other side, and they exploited it. That is, the Russians could rely upon the African nationalists themselves and, later the Cubans to further their own ends while avoiding a direct confrontation with the United States. This policy has already paid rich dividends for the Kremlin in Angola and Mozambique and it holds out further promise in Rhodesia, South-West Africa, and even the Republic itself, if the struggle between the black nationalists and their white rulers in all those countries are not solved in a peaceful manner.

None of this invalidates the strategic importance of South Africa, but it does raise a fundamental question about its defense. While the Republic's ports may be the Soviet Union's ultimate objective, its immediate target is the white government that controls them and its weapon consists of the black nationalists. The question therefore is not so much what should be done about the Soviet threat to the Cape route, an assumed goal of the Kremlin, but rather what should be done about the Soviet threat to the white minority governments in southern Africa, a declared objective of Soviet policy. In the past, defense of the Cape sea lanes tended to be regarded as synonymous with defense of the Pretoria government. Now, the two concepts must be separated carefully, for while the West still retains a serious interest in protecting the Cape, there may be other more palatable and convincing ways of achieving it. But first it is important to look at the other areas of American involvement.

South Africa's minerals, especially gold, chrome, uranium, platinum, manganese, titanium, and vanadium, represent a large proportion of the Western world's total in terms of production and in known reserves. These minerals are important to the West and a certain dependency on the Republic has developed, with chrome, manganese, titanium, and vanadium being of particular importance to the United States armament and aerospace industries. The republic's minerals are produced relatively cheaply with favorable operating and tax conditions provided by the government for American and other foreign mining companies which have played a large part in their development. A sudden cutoff of South African minerals to the United States might cause some dislocation of the aerospace and armament industries although strategic stockpiles exist and are being increased. A more credible scenario would be the gradual throttling of the supply line, such as might happen if racial conflict spreads in the region, resulting in shortages and a rise in prices. This would have two effects. American mining companies, encouraged by the price rise, would develop alternative sources, which do exist, and the federal government would step in and help the development of new supplies through tax concessions and subsidies.

There would be no escaping the fact that the loss of the South African minerals market would mean disruption, perhaps some temporary deficiencies, and certainly higher costs. However, the total removal of South Africa's mineral riches from the world market is unlikely. The Soviet Union has adequate supplies of its own and although it might be interested in denying, or limiting, the amount on the free market, it would not have direct control over the resources of South Africa even if there were a pro-Soviet black government in control. The republic's minerals are its principal source of foreign exchange and it seems highly improbable that any government in Pretoria, whatever its racial or political complexion, would refuse to trade with the West for ideological reasons. Neither Mozambique nor Angola— black, Marxist, and friendly to the Soviet Union—have adopted such an attitude. South Africa's minerals, therefore, are a crucial resource for the West but not, I think, an indispensable one.

The American business stake in South Africa, though naturally important to the companies and individuals concerned, is relatively small. The investment by businesses from the United States is $1.75 billion, a little over 1 percent of their worldwide total; annual trade amounts to just over $2 billion, again about 1 percent of the total. Admittedly, the return on investment, especially in the mining industry, has been high, and the balance of trade is heavily in the United States' favor, American exports being worth twice the value of goods imported from South Africa. However, profitability has dropped since the recession hit South Africa and the American business stake in black Africa—notably with oil-rich Nigeria—is now growing faster than its stake in the white south. (Britain, with double the amount invested in the Republic and a shaky domestic economy, is much more committed than the United States or indeed any other nation that trades with South Africa.) The question about the economic involvement of the United States is not so much over whether or not it represents a vital national interest—it does not—but whether it can be used as a lever for meaningful change or, if it cannot, should it be employed as a sanction.

The last specific area of American interest centers on

the desire for stability in southern Africa which would allow peaceful, evolutionary change to take place, thus minimizing the growth of Soviet influence. This problem involves the nature of the United States relationship with black Africa and, equally important, a proper understanding of the swiftly moving forces now at work in the southern portion of the continent. The old days, when there appeared to be endless amounts of time to solve the racial problems of the region, have gone. The white buffer protecting South Africa has been partially dismantled and the remaining nations—Rhodesia and South-West Africa—will soon be removed. The Soviets and the Cubans are engaged and while they can be expected to exercise caution in view of the strength of the South African state and because they are unlikely to find such a perfect combination of circumstances as they stumbled on in Angola, they are not going to withdraw as long as legitimate African nationalist movements seek their help and the potential for revolution exists.

Much depends, however, on how one rates the urgency of the deepening crisis both on South Africa's borders and inside the citadel. Some analysts argue that it is too early to take sides; the South African government is strong, determined, and here to stay for a long time. Others stress that now is the time to act, to become involved and, inevitably, to choose an ally; any further delay or trying to play both ends against the middle will weaken United States credibility and its role as the honest broker when the struggle does come. It seems to me that the latter interpretation of current realities is the more accurate though I think there are severe limitations on the capacity of the United States to guide events in Africa.

The critical factor in the search for a policy is to determine the extent of the threat to southern African stability. The South Africans assert that Soviet imperialism is entering a dangerously aggressive stage in Africa and that the Western alliance should support the republic as the most effective buffer against communism. The Carter administration, rightly I think, does not ignore the Soviet Union's desire to extend its influence wherever it can in Africa, but it believes the threat is overrated and, more importantly, that it is the inequalities engrained in South Africa's apartheid that offer Moscow the most effective means of implementing its policies. Vice President Mondale, at his meeting with Mr. Vorster in Vienna in May 1977, said: "We believe that perpetuating an unjust system is the surest incentive to increasing Soviet influence." The implication of this statement and his subsequent comment about the need for "full political participation" by all the races in South Africa is that there are other ways of checking Soviet aggrandisement than the old way of a de facto alliance between the United States and the white government in Pretoria.

There appear to be three options open to policymakers in the United States. First disengagement, on the grounds that since American interests are not vital and, moreover, the United States lacks the power and the inclination to resolve the crisis, the best thing to do is to get out before the situation deteriorates even further. Second, gentle pressure could be brought to bear by American businessmen, diplomats, and other contacts, with the aim of persuading the South African government to adopt a more humane and receptive attitude toward the aspirations of its non-white population. This option is a refined version of NSSM option 2 which guided policy in the Nixon era. Finally, a much tougher policy could be adopted toward Pretoria than hitherto, involving economic, financial, diplomatic and political pressures.

There are, of course, more extreme courses of action possible, such as outright support, including military assistance, for either the white government in Pretoria or its black opponents in the South African liberation movements. However, neither of these seems to be a realistic choice. American domestic restraints, in the post-Vietnam and post-Watergate era, would be overwhelming. It is difficult imagining Congress, itself representing a complex interplay of racial interests, either allowing the lifting of the arms embargo against the South African government or sanctioning arms shipments to the black nationalist organizations. Strong support for the whites would alienate the whole of black Africa and play into the hands of the Russians; a powerful commitment to the blacks would suggest that the whites have no role to play at all and would also necessitate making a choice from the broad array of black leaders. Either option would mean that the United States had decided what the best solution to South Africa's problems should be and was taking measures to impose it.

It is necessary to look at the political backdrop in South Africa against which the policy of the United States would be applied. The Afrikaner-dominated Republic of South Africa is preparing itself for the physical and psychological siege which it expects to intensify as Rhodesia and South-West Africa pass under black control and as Africa steps up diplomatic and military pressure against the last bastion of white rule on the continent. Nevertheless, it seems to me that the Republic is entering a new and critical phase in its turbulent history, one in which the old rivalry between white and black nationalisms will become fully engaged and that peace will not come until the issue is resolved. If this is true, then it is an equally critical moment for foreign policy-makers, especially those in the United States where, by a strange coincidence, a president deeply committed both to human rights and to black aspirations has arrived in the White House.

"We know of no great revolution which might not have been prevented by compromise early and graciously made," Thomas Babington Macaulay, the British historian, wrote in 1828. Many people of all races in South Africa say the time has come for meaningful change in their society. But how much time is there? How long before the process of evolution is overtaken and swallowed by revolution? Estimates from each end of the political spectrum in the republic vary but, surprisingly, not a great deal. A decade at the most is the consensus. After that, if nothing happens, the deluge. Assuming the full length of the time-span, the last segments of the buffer zone will have turned black; the Nationalist Party will still be entrenched in power in Pretoria and Jimmy Carter could be in the White House for over half the period.

South Africa has been buffeted by a number of setbacks recently. Vorster's détente strategy with Zambia failed, the Angolan military campaign was defeated, the economy went into deep recession. The international community refused to recognize the independence of the Transkei and Bophuthatswana and the validity of the South African-sponsored elections in Namibia. Then, the United Nations' arms embargo became mandatory. The most serious challenge, however, came not from outside but from within. The black students' revolt on June 16, 1976, rapidly turned into a challenge not only for the totality of government policy but also for the basis on which its authority rests. The upheavals confirmed one significant trend and revealed another. They demonstrated how politicized South African blacks, especially the younger generation, had become; and they showed that polarization of forces, distancing white from white, black from black, and both groups from each other, was taking place. Those two trends will be of critical importance in the future because black politicization will determine the strength of black pressures and the general polarization will determine whether those pressures express themselves in an evolutionary or revolutionary form.

The two poles are clearly defined. On the right stands the Nationalist party comprising nearly all the Afrikaners and many of the English-speaking people. For them, apartheid remains the answer. Coloreds and Indians—both minorities vis-à-vis the blacks and the whites—will have their own parliaments and minigovernments and will be able to consult on national issues with the whites at cabinet level. But they will not be integrated into the whites' political system nor will they have the power to stop measures which they regard as objectionable. For the blacks, the Bantustan plan will continue to unfold, encouraging independence for the tribal areas but not significantly increasing the parsimonious amount of land or resources allotted to them. (In other words, the whites, coloreds, and Indians will retain 87 percent of the country.) Urban blacks, roughly 50 percent of the total African population of 18 million, will have to express themselves politically as citizens of these tribal homelands, regardless of where they live or work, but will be given better social and economic conditions and allowed a certain measure of municipal self-government in their segregated townships.

On the left are the blacks who want the apartheid structures dismantled and full political rights granted to all South Africans in a united country: in short, majority rule. They offer no special protection for minorities apart from a universal bill of rights, but they acknowledge that groups such as the whites and Indians would continue to wield a disproportionate influence through their skills and economic power. Like the Nationalist government, they oppose the concepts of federalism, confederalism and partition. Black leaders would agree to sit around a table and talk to their white rulers about their demands but no one has asked them to do so. Meanwhile, the banned nationalist movements in exile are preparing for war and the black youth inside the country continues to simmer with discontent over the government's separate development policies.

A middleground still exists in South African politics, and it is composed of blacks and whites of goodwill who see the perils ahead and urgently want to redress the ills of their society.

The political forces of the middleground include the white liberal party (the Progressive Federal party) which believes in dropping apartheid and moving, by way of a qualified franchise, to a fully integrated political system. There are main Coloured and Indian political parties which have rejected the government's new constitutional proposals. Gatsha Buthelezi is a Zulu leader who retains his Bantustan platform (KwaZulu) but refuses to accept the homeland independence the government has offered and who speaks for a large following of urban blacks, not all of them by any means Zulus. Other prominent black leaders as well as probably a majority of the working people in the urban areas are followers of moderate policy. Among the whites there are Harry Oppenheimer, the head of South Africa's mining colossus, Anglo-American, and many other important industrialists and businessmen. Most of the English-language newspapers, the Roman Catholic and Anglican churches (but not the Afrikaners' Dutch Reformed Churches), and some of the universities also support this approach.

It would be wrong to imply that these groups share

identical views on their country's future. But they are united on the basics of change: an end to the Bantustan policy, the repeal of all discriminatory legislation, a more equitable share for non-whites in South African society, a meaningful participation by all races in the central political process, and the need for a national convention where leaders representing all South Africa would meet to decide how these reforms could be implemented. While all demand change in the Republic as much as the black South Africans themselves, there is no reason to believe that any insist on either revolutionary methods or a revolutionary outcome unless it becomes clear that there is no other alternative.

This group is important because it provides a focus for Western policy-makers. This is not to say the middle-ground itself is a powerful political force, a viable alternative to the might of Afrikaner and African nationalisms. It is not. But it is just possible that it could provide an evolutionary mechanism, of necessity a transitional device, until power between the two major forces is more evenly balanced. For the West as well as the African states, it is the logical group to address, assuming the extreme options of supporting one principal or the other are rejected. For those who doubt that this is the case, the words of the late Robert Sobukwe, the president of the banned Pan-Africanist Congress, the most radical of the South African nationalist movements, may be persuasive. If the Nationalist government, he said during an interview in December, 1976, were to make three concessions to the blacks—permit them unfettered home ownership in the townships, put an end to job reservation whereby Africans are restricted to certain menial categories of work, and give them some hope of political participation in the future—it would defuse black unrest at a stroke. Sobukwe's own political beliefs were more radical than these demands but he was careful to distinguish between what he aspired to and what the African masses would be content with.

Finally, why should South Africa's center prove to be any more effective than those who tried to find a middle way in places like Algeria, Angola, Mozambique and Rhodesia? There is no certainty that it will; it may fall apart like the others but there are grounds for support- ing it while there is still a chance. The battle lines be- tween white and black are not yet fully drawn up; even the government—or powerful elements within it—may think again if the consequences of its actions can be more graphically pointed out which, in simple language, means pressure. Then, although South Africa houses two conflicting nationalisms, it also possesses a sophisti- cated industrialized economy in which white and black have become indispensable to each other. This affects the Afrikaners, 90 percent of whom are now urbanized, as much as the Africans. So, while there is no metro- politan power to make the ultimate fateful decisions when the going gets rough, there is at least the internal and highly visible factor of mutual economic depend- ency at play.

Against this setting, the various policy options open to the United States can be examined. Disengagement sounds tempting to people tired of foreign involvements and perplexed by the political and racial intricacies of the South African situation. But true disengagement would surely mean the withdrawal of the business inter- ests of the United States, which, while small in the American context, are of great importance to the South African economy. Allowing business to go on as usual, including access to the American financial market, while ignoring the political and diplomatic implications, would smack of collusion with Pretoria and encourage black African states to think that Washington had reverted to its old policy. The alternative, a pull-out by American firms, would almost certainly not be condoned by Congress and would be physically difficult to accomplish. Also it would be hard for the United States as a superpower to turn a blind eye to a deteriorating crisis and for President Carter, a man who has made human rights a central plank of his foreign policy, to wash his hands of South Africa even if he wanted to.

Why not, then, apply persuasion of the reformist option, using business and other contacts to persuade the South African government to improve the social and economic conditions of the blacks at a considerably more rapid pace? President Banda, the only African head of state to have diplomatic relations with the republic, once approvingly summed up this approach as "killing apartheid with kindness." There are, I think, three major criticisms of this option. First, it has been partially tried through private pressure on American companies and, although working conditions of black labor have been improved and black wages have been increased considerably, the worst aspects of apartheid remain intact and show no signs of being removed. Second, this policy would need much more time than is available to prove whether it was going to be effective or not. And finally, the people who are pleading for orderly and peaceful change, those forces in the middleground which probably include a majority of the black workers themselves, do not want it because the results, in their view, would be too little, too late.

That leaves us with the pressure option. There is no guarantee that it will work. The forces of black politicization and racial polarization in South Africa may already be too far advanced for compromise. But, as the seventies draw to a close, it seems to be the only moral as well as practicable course open to the United States government.

Much of the Carter administration's Africa policy is still not formulated, but it is clear that the principle of using pressure against Pretoria, if the South African government continues on its apartheid course, has been endorsed. Equally important, Washington has begun to reshape its policies in black Africa in order to achieve a better balance and avoid the charge of maintaining double standards north and south of the Zambezi river. Carter's government inherited close relationships with Zaire and Ethiopia, countries saddled with dictatorial, repressive, and corrupt regimes, which received arms supplies and other forms of military assistance from the United States. Military aid has been greatly reduced, allowing the administration to view these countries with a new degree of critical detachment. Carter has also made a point of speaking out against African leaders guilty of flagrant breaches of human rights, such as the murderous Idi Amin of Uganda, against whom the United States imposed a total trade embargo in 1978.

A policy involving pressure immediately begs three questions. What is the desired aim of such a policy? What kind of pressures are envisioned? What effect are they likely to have? On the first question, I would part company with the apparent drift of President Carter's policy which, if Vice President Mondale's and Ambassador Andrew Young's statements are accepted as its formulation, endorses majority rule—that is, black rule—as the final objective. There are a number of flaws in this posture. First, it suggests that the United States is dictating a solution to someone else's problem, an intimate and unwarrantable interference in a foreign country's internal affairs. Second, Washington is placing itself on one side of the conflict, the black side, without showing any real desire to put enough weight behind it to ensure that the objective is secured. There is a grave danger of raising South African blacks' expectations, as well as those of the United States' friends in Africa, but not being capable of fulfilling them. If the United States was preparing to take punitive action against South Africa— by imposing an oil embargo or supplying arms for the black nationalists, among other things, then there would be less chance of recrimination because, if the policy failed, Washington could genuinely say it had done its best. But these are almost certainly not the sort of pressures that the Administration has in mind. Third, the concept of majority rule, and the implications it has for the whites in South Africa through their reading of events in the rest of Africa after majority rule was granted, has come to be resisted even by the most moderate and understanding people. South Africa's whites may eventually be persuaded to accept black rule, but a more subtle approach, while they are locked in their current state of fearfulness and defiance, is necessary. Loose talk of "majority rule" merely strengthens the reactionaries and frightens off the moderates. It is not as if it was not clear what the majority of South Africans want: full political participation, equality before the law, abolition of racially discriminatory legislation, the ending of inequitable labor practices, and so on. But it would be arrogant for anyone foreign to that extraordinarily complex country to prescribe the constitutional remedy. That, surely, is the prerogative of the South Africans themselves. And whatever they choose— majority rule in a unified state, federalism, confederalism, even partition or apartheid—is their right and should be respected by the world community. The United States should not be specifying ends but means.

The only way in which South Africa's difficulties will be resolved, short of on the battlefield, will be through genuine dialogue between the races. Many people, especially those in the middle-ground, have been calling for this kind of communication for years. Dialogue will not guarantee a peaceful solution but it is the first essential step toward one. It is thus a wholly legitimate objective of policy for a powerful nation like the United States which wants to help but does not want to dictate solutions nor become inextricably involved.

The kind of pressures that could be expected to bring the South African government to its knees are not likely to be applied by the United States. The republic's critical vulnerabilities are its oil supply; certain armaments, notably fighter planes and submarines, a steady and profitable market for its gold, free access to the West's financial institutions, and open trade lanes to the West and Japan. Cutting off South Africa's oil would require the cooperation of Congress and the major oil companies; neither is likely to agree to such a move in the foreseeable future. In order to disrupt the republic's gold revenues—the largest element in its foreign exchange earnings—the use of the metal in the world monetary system would have to be stopped, again an unlikely contingency. The extension of the arms embargo, by making it mandatory at the United Nations, has worried the South African government but not unduly because it is self-sufficient for roughly 75 percent of its needs and can rely on loopholes and freelance arms dealers to make good the deficiency. (The supply of large sophisticated weaponry now poses a problem, however.)

Considering more practical applications, the South Africans most fear the imposition of mandatory economic sanctions, sponsored by the United Nations, of the kind applied to Rhodesia and from which Britain, France and the United States have traditionally shielded them by using their vetoes in the Security Council. Such sanctions, in spite of the likelihood that they would not be very effective, would be regarded as a disaster by Pretoria because they would drive the country further into isolation and give an aura of legitimacy to subsequent hostile actions. There is no sign that the United States is moving to impose a trade embargo on South Africa, and it is probable that this is the last on Washington's list of practicable pressures. The whole process of applying pressure to South Africa is likely to be a slow and cautious one. It is slow because the nature of pressure is such that it cannot be applied overnight. It must be applied cautiously because Washington will be keen to monitor any response and adjust the pressure accordingly. The first phase, the sending of "signals" to the South African government, is already under way. Pretoria has been told in plain terms that the United States will not aid the whites if the South African government's racial policies lead to civil war. The arms embargo has been tightened. Other forms of pressure are being studied. They include discouraging new American investment in South Africa; removing tax credits from American companies which operate in the Republic; encouraging, with financial inducements, development of alternative sources of the minerals South Africa currently supplies to the United States; discouraging American banks making loans to the South African government; reducing diplomatic representation; ending scientific and intelligence links; stopping Export-Import Bank credits for American exports to the republic; and encouraging South Africa's other trading partners, especially Britain, France, West Germany, and Japan, to adopt similar measures. If there is no significant movement toward reform by Pretoria, there is a good chance that some, perhaps all, of these sanctions will gradually be applied.

How effective will these measures be? And what sort of reaction can be expected from South Africa? The levers over which the administration has complete control, including tax credits, or diplomatic representation, are the easiest to exercise. Others, such as seeking other sources of minerals and stopping American bank loans, require time and perhaps legislation. There seems little doubt that in the early stages of the policy the damage inflicted upon the South Africans will be more psychological than physical. But since the republic is a nation highly dependent upon trade and foreign investment, its economy will feel the effects unless the loss brought about by the Americans is made up by someone else, not a likely prospect if the political situation continues to deteriorate and exert its own malign influence upon the drawing power of the South African economy. The key imponderable about the will of the whites will then be closer to resolution: Are they prepared to accept a significant reduction in their standard of living as well as a more dangerous and isolated lifestyle as the price of adhering to their government's racial policies? Only time will provide the answer.

There are indications that the South African government is acutely aware of its predicament and has made some concessions to Western pressures. Pretoria's decision to agree to negotiate with the United States and other Western nations over the future of Namibia was the most dramatic example, but some internal changes also reflect the government's sensitivity. The campaign to eliminate the indignities of "petty apartheid" (by removing discriminatory signs, and opening hotels, libraries, parks, and some forms of transport to blacks, among other things) to give greater municipal powers to the African townships and the rights to buy homes in them, granting the coloreds and Indians their own parliaments, and promises to improve the quality of black education all show that the government knows it has to make an effort to produce a more egalitarian society. A senior government minister asked an American official shortly after Carter's victory at the polls in 1976 what kind of changes did the Americans want in South Africa. It was the right question, but the wrong addressee. It showed the Afrikaners were beginning to think deeply about their future though they had not yet plucked up courage to talk to the right people, their own black and brown countrymen, about it.

It would be unrealistic to expect a complete change of heart by the South African government, however. Pressure may indeed spur the South Africans to press ahead even faster with their apartheid strategy, as many critics of the option have suggested. The facts show that Pretoria remains unbending on the central aspects of apartheid and is relentlessly pursuing its goals with all the energy it can muster. No one who has been to South Africa since the Soweto upheavals can be sanguine about a peaceful outcome. I certainly am not and feel that a racial conflict is a strong possibility in the not-so-distant future, destroying both the whites' dream of an apartheid paradise and the blacks' vision of an African utopia. The greatest pressures of all will come from inside, not outside, the country. And the result, I fear, will be a bloodily executed partition. This, however, does not relieve the United States and other interested parties of the moral responsibility for using the limited power that they possess. The confused and worried millions in the center of the South African maelstrom want pressure put on their government since they lack the means of applying it themselves. They constitute the last fragile hope for peace, and their plea should not be ignored.

BIBILOGRAPHY

1. Rhoodie, Nic, ed. *South African Dialogue*. New York: McGraw-Hill Book Co., 1972.
2. Thompson, Leonard and Jeffrey Butler, eds. *Change in Contemporary South Africa*. Berkeley and Los Angeles: University of California Press, 1975.
3. Wilson, Monica, and Leonard Thompson, eds. *The Oxford History of South Africa*. New York: Oxford University Press, 1971.
4. de Klerk, William. *The Puritans in Africa*. London: Rex Collings, 1975.
5. Barker, James P. *South Africa's Foreign Policy, 1945 to 1970*. London: Oxford University Press, 1973.
6. Butler, Jeffrey, Robert I. Rotberg, and John Adams. *The Black Homelands of South Africa*. Berkeley and Los Angeles: University of California Press, 1977.
7. El-Khawas, Mohammad A., and Barry Cohen. *The Kissinger Study of Southern Africa*. Westport, Connecticut: Lawrence Hill & Co., 1976.
8. Adam, Herbert. *Modernizing Racial Domination: South Africa's Political Dynamics*. Berkeley and Los Angeles: University of California Press, 1971.
9. Moodie, T. Dunbar. *The Rise of Afrikanerdom: Power, Apartheid, and the Afrikaner Civil Religion*. Berkeley and Los Angeles: University of California Press, 1975.
10. Rogers, Barbara. *White Wealth and Black Poverty: American Investment in Southern Africa*. Westport, Connecticut: Greenwood Press, 1976.
11. Hoagland, James. *South Africa: Civilizations in Conflict*. Boston: Houghton-Mifflin, 1972.
12. South African Institute of Race Relations. *A Survey of Race Relations*. Johannesburg: South Africa.

13. Khoapa, B. A., ed. *The Black Review, 1972*. Durban, South Africa: Black Community Programs, 1973.
14. Mbanjwa, Thoko, ed. *The Black Review, 1974/75*. Durban, South Africa: Black Community Programs, 1975.
15. Legum, Colin. *African Contemporary Record*. New York: Afrikaner Publishing Co.
16. Paton, Alan. *Too Late the Phalarope*. New York: Charles Scribner's Sons, 1953.
17. de St. Jorre, John. *A House Divided: South Africa's Uncertain Future*. Washington, D.C.: Carnegie Endowment for International Peace, 1977.
18. Gerhart, Gail. *Black Power in South Africa: The Evolution of an Ideology*. Berkeley: University of California, 1978.

Human Rights and American Foreign Policy
The Case of Iran

MARVIN ZONIS

The welfare of the people must be carefully guarded by the king as that of his bodyguard. . . . It is through the people that the country is made prosperous, for the revenues are earned by the people, who remain settled and prosperous if given what is rightfully theirs. Therefore, let there be no place in your heart for extortion; the dynasty of kings who recognize rights endures long and becomes old, but the dynasty of extortions swiftly perishes, because fair treatment means prosperity, and extortion means a depopulated land. . . . The sages say that the well-spring of thriving conditions and of gladness in the world is a just king, while the source of desolation and misery is a king who is an oppressor.[1]

A prince of the Caspian region advising his son on the principles of ruling, 1082 A.D.

Certainly we are concerned with the matter of the trials. . . . One must realize that this has been a grass roots revolution up to the stage of the victory, that is, all the casualties have been sustained on the side of the people. That means all of the people on the side of the Shah, admirals, generals, and all the

131

people in SAVAK, are alive and well, and they have arms in their hands. So in order to cope with that, the revolutionists must take certain actions.

It is undoubtedly the case that the form of the trials which are being held is not in exact accordance with Islamic law, but it must be understood that this is a revolutionary process. . . . It is unfair to call it brutality while the Shah's brutalities and repression and so on are considered something else—such as an iron hand; you know, killing 65,000 people within a year.[2]

> Shahriar Rouhani, Spokesman for the Interim Committee to oversee the activities of the Iranian diplomatic corps in the United States, 1979.

HUMAN RIGHTS

Iran has become an increasingly important and fascinating case for American students of human rights as well as for those concerned with revolutions. The nearly 38-year rule of the Shah of Iran was brought to an end in early 1979 by his departure for an "extended vacation" abroad after a massive, nationwide and essentially nonviolent uprising against him and the political order he created. Much to the amazement of outside observers, and to many in Iran as well, the "Revolution of 1977-1979" succeeded despite huge increases in oil revenues available to the Shah, his creation of powerful and ruthless security forces—both secret police and the armed forces, the ardent support of foreign powers, in particular the United States, and his own political skills learned through decades of day-to-day control over the entire state.

This paper does not attempt a history or analysis of that revolution. But it does attempt an examination of the role that the concern for human rights played in the prerevolutionary years in Iran, in the revolution itself, and in that phase of the on-going revolution marked by the departure of the Shah. It is clear that a variety of economic, political, and social forces opposed the Shah.[3] Concern for human rights was articulated by Iranians as well as foreigners in terms of Western secular concepts or Shi'ite Islamic concepts or in "a new Islamic idiom" which "endeavored to integrate the fruits of modern learning with traditional belief."[4]

Certainly the widespread concern for the violation of human rights by the Shah was an important source of this opposition to him and one of the principal ways in which that opposition—irrespective of its ultimate source—was expressed. Without, then, attempting any analysis of the revolution here, it is clear that an examination of "human rights" is an essential part of any larger attempt to understand the Revolution of 1977-1979.

THE IRAN-U.S. LINK AND HUMAN RIGHTS

That the revolution was successful in ousting the Shah is startling given the image of increasing power and control which he managed to project during the 1970s. The Shah of Iran had overseen and largely determined the fate of his nation since first assuming the royal office in 1941. He had remained in office in a country and region known for its political turmoil, ardently defending the monarchy in an age devoted to notions of democracy and socialism, as well as effecting a transformation of Iran economically, socially, and militarily. In his foreign policy he was determined to maintain close ties with Western Europe and especially the United States when other rulers had proclaimed their solidarity with the third world. All this made the Shah and Iran the focus of close American attention and all too often awe (which in turn disheartened his own people). The new role of Iran as a major world supplier of petroleum and the principal customer for American arms also gave the United States the justification to support the monarchy.

But yet another issue led to the urgency with which Iranian affairs were considered in the United States and which in turn contributed to increasing domestic discontent. Since 1971, Iran had become the subject of international concern over questions of the violation of human rights. A growing number of compelling and often dramatic reports of the use of torture on political prisoners received wide circulation. Responsibility for such torture was attached to Iran's secret police—the State Information and Intelligence Organization, commonly known as Savak from the acronym of its Persian name. Savak activities were publicized as pervasive inside Iran while accounts of their activities among Iranian student and emigre groups in Europe and the United States were claimed by the Shah himself.

Reports of the torture of prisoners were most frequently given by a number of Iranians who were the victims of the Iranian secret police, Savak. Most notable, perhaps, were the accounts given by the former Associate Professor of English Literature at the University of Tehran, Reza Baraheni. He emigrated to the United States after being held for 102 days in 1973 in the Komite prison operated in Tehran by Savak and the National Iranian Police. His many English language accounts of his incarceration and torture were extremely effective in eliciting widespread concern over Iran within the United States.[5] In addition, sentiments against the Shah were expressed by the Iranian students in the United States.[6] (More students from Iran were studying in American institutions of higher education— from 30,000 to 75,000 depending on whose statistics one accepts—than from any other country. Many of them belonged to organizations committed to political change in Iran.) Their organizations publicized reports of torture and political struggles in Iran that were not carried in the American media.[7] A few international agencies, such as Amnesty International[8] and the International Commission of Jurists,[9] also have issued reports critical of Iran for the treatment of political prisoners.

These reports, coupled with news of terrorist activities in Iran and public statements by the Shah himself, led the House Committee on International Relations to request the Secretary of State to supply information on the "observance of and respect for human rights and fundamental freedoms" in Iran pursuant to the International Security Assistance and Arms Export Control Act of 1976 which ties American security assistance to the observance of such rights.[10] Subsequently the Committee held hearings on human rights in Iran.[11]

But there were other reasons for the special American concern about Iran. Fundamentally, these reasons had to do with the long-standing relationship which existed between the United States and Iran, and, more particularly, the Shah. That relationship began to take its current form with the overthrow of Prime Minister Mohammad Mossadegh through the active participation of the C.I.A. and the return of the Shah from a hasty flight to Rome in August 1953. Following the reestablishment of kingly authority, the three basic components of American-Iranian relations were established.

First, the United States became involved in the economy of Iran. Directly the United States began making cash grants to Iran to meet any annual deficit in the government's budget (a policy that continued until 1963). In addition, the United States made grants and loans of nearly $1 billion for economic development. Indirectly, the United States became involved in 1954 when a consortium of American oil companies bought a 40 percent share in Iranian oil production.

Immediately after the return of the Shah in 1953, Iran was placed under martial law with a military government headed by General Fazlollah Zahedi. The general and the Shah began receiving sizeable quantities of American military assistance along with equally impressive numbers of American military personnel to train the armed forces of Iran in their use. In 1957 the United States helped the Shah establish his centralized secret police force and the C.I.A. trained Savak for their counterintelligence role. By 1964, the United States had supplied Iran with nearly $1 billion of military aid.[12]

Following 1964, President Johnson agreed to provide Iran with foreign military sales credits and to allow outright purchases of military equipment by Iran. But the major change in America's security relationship with Iran was made in May of 1972, when President Nixon agreed to sell Iran the technologically advanced F-14 or F-15 aircraft and, in the future, any conventional weapons system it wished to buy without review by the departments of State or Defense.

After the fourfold petroleum price increases in 1973 and 1974, no reexamination of this policy was carried out. The government of Iran went on an arms-buying spree the implications of which—in terms of economic, strategic, and tactical considerations—are only now being understood. In the words of a United States Senate study:

Iran is the largest single purchaser of U.S. military equipment. Government-to-government military sales to Iran increased over seven-fold from $524 million in Fiscal Year 1972 to $3.91 billion in FY 1974, slackening off a little to $2.6 billion in FY 1975. The preliminary sales estimate for FY 1976 is $1.3 billion. Sales in the 1972-1976 period totalled $10.4 billion. The number of official and private American citizens in Iran, a large percentage of whom are involved in military programs, has also increased from approximately 15,000-16,000 in 1972 to 24,000 in 1976; it could easily reach 50,000-60,000 or higher by 1980.[13]

The third basic component of American involvement in Iran was rooted in the Iranian economy and armed forces and entailed close political cooperation between the two countries. The political relationship which existed was undoubtedly not more pervasive than that which existed with other states informally allied to the United States. But there is a sense, in the case of Iran, of a special link, of a particular political resonance which implicated the United States in Iranian affairs. This resonance was rooted in a set of beliefs which were widely shared in Iranian politics; shared by the most ardent devotees of the regime as well as by its most vociferous opponents. The beliefs were that Iran occupied a special place in American international policy. The American government developed an exceptional capacity to influence the course of domestic politics in Iran. The ability of the United States to influence Iran was "proved" by the Shah's adopting policies for Iran which so clearly served American interest. He refused to join the oil embargo and expressed the willingness to "protect" the sea lanes of the Persian Gulf following the British withdrawal in 1971, to give but two examples. The government of Iran and, in particular, the Shah became extremely sensitive to the currents of American political opinion.

That Iran played a special role in American thinking was "demonstrated" by the appointment of ex-C.I.A. director Richard Helms and by that of his successor, William H. Sullivan, so active in southeast Asian affairs, as Ambassadors to Iran as well as by America's carte blanche military sales.

The sensitivity of the Shah and his government to American political opinion was demonstrated by the anxiety generated in Iranian governing circles when President Carter failed to respond to the congratulatory telegram sent by the Shah on the occasion of his election victory in November, 1976. That fact became widely known and Tehran was buzzing with interpretations of President Carter's "obvious" dissatisfaction with the Shah and the consequences for Iran which would likely follow. When President Carter received the foreign diplomatic corps, Iranian newspapers covered their front pages with a picture of the president greeting Ambassador Ardeshir Zahedi. Iranian readers were assured that the president told Zahedi that he wished to reciprocate the Shah's friendly message. It was not until the second week of February, 1977, however, that the Iranian press was able to report the receipt of a formal reply to the Shah's message. With almost audible relief, one press report began its story: "President Carter, in his first direct communication with the Shahanshah, has affirmed his commitment to a firm friendship with Iran." [14] But the anxiety was only slightly mitigated, for the press also reported that the cable stated that "There are bound to be challenges to our common objectives, but there are also reasons for optimism and progress." [15] The ambiguities of that phrase maintained the doubts. The relevance of this incident seems clear. The United States was deeply involved in the economic, political, and military affairs of Iran. It possessed a variety of means for the exercise of influence over the policies of the government of Iran. The entire politically aware segments of Iran's population were extremely sensitive to nuances in American policy.

To many in Iran, it appeared that the inauguration of President Carter would initiate an attitude toward the Shah like that which was developed following the inauguration of President Kennedy, who was allegedly dissatisfied with the Shah's policy on human rights. Carter's clear concern for human rights also was understood as directly applicable to the rule of the Shah. This perception certainly emboldened segments of the intelligentsia in Iran to believe that the time was right for protesting the increasingly repressive regime of the Shah. And in a complementary process, the Shah seems to have believed much the same thing—that President Carter had delivered a clear statement of a new policy which he expected from the Shah. Again, partly in response to his perception, and also to a variety of other factors which need not be given here, the Shah's response to the initial protests by the intelligentsia seemed equivocating and indecisive. This only served to further embolden the opposition within Iran. Thus, in 1977, more than 50 lawyers announced the formation of an independent committee to monitor the judicial system. A larger number of playwrights, novelists, and poets reformed the Writers' Association of Iran and sent an open letter to Prime Minister Hoveyda criticizing censorship of their works. A large number of "bazaaris" formed a Society of Merchants, Traders and Craftsmen to protest government interference in the commercial life of Iran. They also condemned, publicly, the Shah's single political party, the *Rastakhiz*.

What is now clear is the incredible restraint exercised by the opposition throughout 1977 and even during the peak year of revolutionary activity, 1978. While arms were readily available, having been smuggled into Iran in greater and greater numbers as the revolution progressed, they were simply not put in the service of the revolution. To the contrary, those arms which were used were used by the regime against its opponents. Many thousands were killed in street demonstrations and rioting, and, undoubtedly, tens of thousands were wounded. All the while, hundreds and thousands of others were arrested and held without trial in mass detentions.

Since the ouster of the Shah in early 1979, the expectations of many Iranians and sympathetic foreign observers for a more humane and just society have not been met. The revolution has been dominated by Ayatollah Khomeini and a group of Shi'ite clerics and laymen devoted to his theocratic vision, although that is clearly not the result which inspired many, if not most, of those who participated in the revolution. The so-called revolutionary tribunals have executed at least 250 officials of the former regime as well as a few businessmen with no official roles and have arrested some few thousand. Nevertheless, the old instruments of repression have collapsed or been disbanded by the revolutionaries. Savak has been effectively destroyed. The extent of power which the Ayatollah can exercise in comparison to the Shah has been dramatically reduced.

Perhaps more menacing to human rights is the fact that political power has been centralized in a small clique around Ayatollah Khomeini. Among other activities, they are drafting a new constitution in secret. The provisions it will make for the protection of the rights of such minorities as non-Persian ethnic and linguistic groups, as well as the religious minorities of Christians, Jews, and Zoroastrians is unclear. It is not likely to satisfy the demands for at least cultural autonomy voiced by the Kurds, Turkomens, Azeris, Arabs, and others.

The political system remains in flux, and strong voices are being raised in exception to the narrow clerical vision which Ayatollah Khomeini and his followers are attempting to impose on Iran; voices which come not only from the westernized, secular, and liberal intelligentsia, but from other Ayatollahs, followers of Dr. Ali Shari'ati, Marxist and Islamic guerilla groups, and the minorities. Iran seems poised on the brink of further dramatic changes; changes whose shape and outcome cannot now be determined. But without meaning to condone the executions and other revolutionary excesses which have been committed in its name, the period since the revolution cannot be equated in any significant way with Iran from 1971 to 1978.

COMPONENTS OF HUMAN RIGHTS

"Human rights" in the fullest sense of the term refers first, to the nature of the legal and judicial systems. Second, it entails a notion of "positive" human rights or the benefits which are received by the population. Finally, the term also entails a notion of the distribution and nature of political power within any given system.

The debate over human rights in Iran both under the Shah and the Ayatollah has focussed on only two of the three components of that concept. Critics have accused the regime of the Shah and the revolutionary regime of violating the human rights of dissidents as well as of the violation of Iranian law and international standards of due process by the use of torture and summary execution (Iran is a signatory to a variety of international declarations on human rights). Spokesmen for the government of the Shah responded by pointing to the elaborate programs of social and economic reforms enacted since the implementation of the "White Revolution" in 1963. The dissidents were accused of being either "red revolutionaries" or "black revolutionaries" attempting to impede the realization of the constantly broadened reforms, the "Shah-people revolution." Spokesmen for the Ayatollah, like Shahriar Rouhani, legitimize their executions on the basis of the need to eliminate counter-revolution or to impose their version of Islamic justice (a version it needs be added which is very little shared by most significant Islamic thinkers in Iran).

However, critics have overlooked the fact that Iranians have lost the right to participate in their own political system, to affect the allocation and distribution of resources through the political process. And what a shortcoming that is. For the Iranian Gross National Product is rapidly approaching $50 billion per year. In short, to be without influence over that vast government bureaucracy or the revolutionary committee surrounding Ayatollah Khomeini is to be unable to alter the expenditure of 80 percent of the GNP. But is is more than the right to control the allocation of resources and to establish control over the priorities of the budget which is at issue. The fact that the fundamental political liberties: freedom of expression, of assembly, of organization, of participation, have been lost also has been obscured by the more dramatic issue of the torture and execution of political dissidents or representatives of the old regime.

The Issue of Human Rights in the Historical and Cultural Context of Iran

The historical record of Iran reveals that "torture" and "cruel or inhuman punishment" have been applied in Iran since the beginning of its recorded history. The Deputy Minister of Foreign Affairs of Iran made it clear to the British Ambassador in 1838.

> The Monarchs of Persia, as far back as memory reaches, or is preserved in history, have always been despotic over Persian subjects, in like manner over their lives, and property, and families, and reputations, and lands, and goods; so that even if they should order a thousand innocent persons to be put to death, it would be in no one's power to call them to account.[16]

Instances of torture are found in the accounts of every dynasty.[17] But the cruelty with which Shahs treated their subjects did not comprise all the depredations to which the hapless people were subject. They were overwhelmingly peasants, and their landlords also could treat them cruelly.[18]

By the end of the nineteenth century, Iran was in total disarray. The Shah had little power over the country, what control there was being exercised by provincial governors and local chiefs. "Nothing can be more disheartening than the situation," wrote the British Charge d'Affaires. "There is no law, no administration, no army. The poor do not know where to turn for justice; the management of affairs is in the hands of corrupt officials who have bought their posts; and the sums which are supposed to be devoted to the army are absorbed by those through whose hands they pass." [19]

This observation speaks to the key difference between contemporary and past violations of human rights. The Pahlavi regime did not continue an historical system, but centralized repression. The near monopolization of the instruments of violence by the state, the use of new technologies and institutions (such as prisons which were unknown before) and the commitment of these instruments to achieving absolute control over the lives of its people were totally new phenomena in Iran. Before the mid-1960s, for example, Iran was noteworthy for the extent to which its people were allowed freedom of expression, as long as the opinions expressed were not widely or publicly disseminated. Visitors to Iran were struck by the criticisms of politics so freely expressed at Tehran's parties and by the satirical and pointed humor, especially as published in the weekly journal *Tofigh*. That expression was not a new phenomenon. In the mid-nineteenth century, an English traveler noted, "The freedom of speech allowed in Persia is extraordinary; it seems to be a safety valve for the discontent of the people, and seldom leads to any harm. As long as the Iranians *do* nothing, they can *say* what they please." [20] Under the Shah, even this freedom was eliminated. Freedom of expression was not allowed in the 1970s, even when opinions were not widely circulated. The Shah seemed intent on establishing a form of royal absolutism totally different in the pervasiveness and centrality of its social control from the dissolution of central authority of the late nineteenth century.

This intention was not, of course, what the Iranian people had in mind when they joined together in what is now known as the "Constitutional Revolution." In 1906, the Qajar Shah agreed to the implementation of a written constitution which established the formal system of government by which Iran was supposedly ruled, under the Shah, including a bicameral parliament, a cabinet, specified voting, and other human rights and provisions, never enforced, for a form of judicial review by a panel of learned Islamic clerics. But significantly, in the initial phases of the movement, the demands of those "revolutionaries" were aimed not at a parliament but towards the formation of a "House of Justice." And throughout the first decade of this century, the political ferment in Iran was characterized by "a demand for justice."[21] However, the justice which the revolutionaries of 1905 sought was not forthcoming, for the constitution was a flawed document. Virtually every article which limited the power of the state and the monarch, limitations meant to assure the desperately sought justice, allowed the abrogation of such provisions "in the interests of the state."

But more fundamentally, any constitution is valuable to the extent to which the distribution of political power allows the nongoverning population to impose political limitations on the ruler.[22] The history of twentieth-century Iran illustrates the failure of these people. Beginning, particularly, with the rise to power of the father of the present Shah in 1921 and continuing under Mohammad Reza Shah, with mounting intensity, Iranian politics have been marked by the increasing centralization of political power within the state bureaucracies dominated by the Shah. In short, the constitution of Iran, its entire legal structure, became a means for the Shah to govern, an instrument of royal control.

Many reasons can be advanced to account for the power of the Shah, from his brilliance, shrewdness, and toughness, to the support he received from the United States, to the disarray and failures of opposition politicians. While these reasons are all valid, at its base, attention must be focussed on the nature and sources of wealth in Iran. The nongoverning populace of Iran were not able to construct a base of economic resources independent of the state which would have allowed them to withhold such resources from the state in exchange for political concessions or to use the power which such resources would allow to demand such political concessions. A wealthy merchant class did evolve in the late nineteenth and early twentieth centuries, and gained political power under the original constitution. The decisive stage of that 1905-1907 Revolution was the taking of *bast* or sanctuary by some twelve to fourteen thousand merchants on the grounds of the British summer embassy. That move, along with a similar *bast* by Islamic clerics in the city of Qom, was sufficient to overcome the Shah's adamant refusal to grant the desired Constitution.[23]

The crucial change which has occurred in Iran since those simpler days is the alteration of its economic structure, specifically due to the growth of oil. That is, especially since the fourfold price increases of late 1973 and early 1974, Iran has received upwards of $20 billion per year for its oil exports. Those fabulous sums flowed directly to the central treasury of the country and the Shah. This reduced the political resources of Iran's active and growing private entrepreneurs. The result was that the economic importance of those entrepreneurs, along with their political power, was relatively diminished to a point where their capacity to extract political concessions from the regime was effectively eliminated. There were, then, no economic forces independent of the power of the Shah, forces which in the West have been responsible historically for demands for civil liberties.

This is not to suggest that such forces in Iran have been economically destroyed by the state. To the contrary, one aspect of the genius of the Pahlavi political system was that what it took in terms of political power, it returned in the form of economic gain. Thus, while the entrepreneurs became more than ever subject to erratic and often arbitrary interference by the state, their material positions were enhanced beyond even their own wildest expectations of only a few years earlier. The incentive of the middle and upper strata to demand legal protection for their material positions was effectively, if perhaps only temporarily diminished, by the willingness of the state to share its material prosperity with wider and wider sectors of the population.

Thus, concern over political power and civil liberties became the province of a relatively small number of intellectuals. Unfortunately, those Iranian intellectuals were not supported in their demands for civil liberties by the ever more powerful economic bourgeoisie. Rather than joining the cause of the intellectuals to press the state for freedom to pursue their entrepreneurial activities, the state succeeded in coopting the most successful of those entrepreneurs along with many other segments of the population through the economic largesse made possible to it by the burgeoning oil revenues.

There was, of course, one sector of the population which the Shah never succeeded in coopting—the Muslim clergy or ulema. They were the group which ultimately provided the leadership and organizational capacities which made the revolution in 1977 possible. But sadly for those committed to the expansion of human rights in Iran, many of these clerics had different priorities and commitments. That group of the ulema which ultimately became dominant in the great political struggles of 1977 and 1978 was not committed to limiting the power of the state to allow for greater political freedoms. Rather it sought to replace the regime with a new political order dominated by a Shi'ite conception of legitimacy which has proved, at this point, to be far from Western ideals of human rights.

Another key group that took part in the revolution in 1977 was the workers in the southern oil fields. They refused to produce petroleum for export, which shut off the economic basis of the regime and sealed its doom. But this group, as was the case with the ulema, were not committed to achieving Western concepts of human rights. They exercised power at a crucial moment of the revolution. But that was done in the interest of over- throwing the Shah, not in achieving human rights.

OPPOSITION IN THE 1970s

A striking change in the politics of Iran first took place in 1971. Organized political groups were formed which were intensely opposed to the regime and which pos- sessed a sense of the futility of attempting to alter the nature of the state through conventional political chan- nels. The result was an outburst of political terrorism and violence. There had, of course, been groups ard- ently opposed to ruling regimes throughout Iranian his- tory. Many of these groups have engaged in politically motivated violence as well. For example, a number of attempts were made against the Shah, including one in 1949 when he was wounded by shots fired at close range and another as recently as 1965 when a series of rooms in one palace was sprayed by machine gun bullets fired by a member of the Imperial Guards. The Shah escaped injury when the Guardsman was shot down by the Shah's immediate bodyguard.

What differentiated the groups in the 1970s was the number of persons involved, their organization and use of violence against representatives and "agents" of the regime, including Americans, and the inability of the security forces of Iran to extirpate them. It is still difficult to obtain information about these groups other than through the government-controlled media or occasional broadsides from dissidents. There were, it seems, several groups, of which the two most significant were the *Cherikha-yi Fedayi Khalq* (The People's Devoted Guerillas) and the *Sazeman-i Mujahidin-i Khalq* (The Organization of the People's Fighters). The former was widely known as the "Fedayin." It was militantly Marxist and secular in character, committed to the need for revolutionary violence to overthrow the regime of the Shah. The latter group was an outgrowth of the Movement for the Liberation of Iran, organized in the 1960s by Prime Minister Bazergan. Bazergan took issue with the avowedly secular stance of the National Front and formed his movement to effect an Islamic version of a modern, technological society, with political freedoms and civil liberties. The Mujahidin, in turn, split from Bazergan over their growing insistance on the need for armed struggle while yet maintaining the primacy of an Islamic vision.

The first dramatic act of violence occurred on February 8, 1971, when an attack was made on the headquarters of the gendarmerie in the small town of Siakhal in Gilan province of northern Iran. Two guerillas were reported slain in the attack along with the downing of a government helicopter. The security forces acted with dispatch announcing the discovery of a network of guerrillas throughout the province. On March 17 of the same year, it was announced that 13 persons were executed for membership in the "Siakhal group."

Despite the apparent efficiency with which the security forces were able to respond, the violence continued.

Most notably, on April 7, 1971, General Farsiou, the head of the Military Tribunal and, thus, the chief judge responsible for the trial of political dissidents, was shot and killed as he left his home. The regime finally decided it had to impose strict security in the fall of 1971. At that time, the Shah had scheduled the grandiose celebrations, centered in southern, rural Iran outside of Shiraz, to commemorate the 2500th anniversary of the founding of the Achaemenid dynasty. Scores of heads of foreign states were invited to attend and to spend up to a week in an elegantly constructed tent city near the ruins of Persepolis. Perhaps no other occasion could have presented political dissidents with a more opportune moment for the embarrassment, if not worse, of the regime. In response, the security forces of Iran imposed a vigorous and near total military control of the entire country.

The regime did succeed in avoiding any untoward incidents, but, with the departure of the eminent foreign visitors, it lifted the extraordinary security precautions. The violence resumed. Again, reliable data on "terrorist" or "guerilla" activities are difficult to obtain. The regime sought to minimize such activities while the guerillas sought to maximize the effects of their actions. What is certain is that such activities continued—bank robberies, bombings, and the assassination of military and Savak officers have occurred with regularity since 1971. Moreover, Americans were involved in the violence. On May 21, 1975, two American Army colonels were machine gunned in their car, while on August 28, 1976, three American employees of Rockwell International were similarly executed.

The security forces of Iran responded to the violence with increasing stringency. "Headquarters" of "terrorists" were discovered, particularly in Tehran but in other cities as well. Efforts to capture the "terrorists" frequently resulted in shootings wherein up to two dozen "guerillas" were killed. Many others were captured in security sweeps. At the trials scores of prisoners were found guilty and sentenced to death or long prison terms.[24] Moreover, Savak began to pursue individuals deemed politically reprehensible with a special intensity. It was in the context of such general political control that intellectuals were arrested. For example, Reza Baraheni and the eminent playwright and author, Dr. Gholem Hossein Sa'edi, were imprisoned.

According to the Iranian law of the time, all persons charged with political crimes—a very broad category—were subject to military justice. For this purpose, the State Security and Intelligence Organization was defined as a military organization and Savak representatives were considered military magistrates. Thus persons who were arrested for alleged political crimes passed through a totally secret judicial process distinct from the conventional channels of the Ministry of Justice and the system of civil courts.

The exact number of political prisoners taken is not known. Iranian dissidents and their supporters claimed that up to 200,000 were incarcerated in Iranian jails; Amnesty International put the figure in the neighborhood of 20,000.[25] The Shah himself, on "Meet the Press" in May of 1976, claimed that less than 3000 persons were political prisoners in Iran and that all of these were guilty of carrying out acts of political violence. In his testimony to the United States House Committee investigating human rights in Iran, the Assistant Secretary of State for Near Eastern and South Asian Affairs, Alfred L. Atherton, suggested that

There is no precise definition of the term "political

prisoner" in the Iranian context, but there may well
be . . . perhaps 100 to 150 . . . persons who have been
detained, arrested, or punished for their beliefs or
opinions but who have neither used nor advocated
violence.

. . . I am reasonably certain that the large majority
of prisoners who have gone through the military
court system were convicted for involvement in
planning or carrying out violent acts against the
security of the state, or overtly engaged in acts of
terrorism, or were associated in some way with the
terrorists. The number of such people in prison
today is probably in the range of 2,800 to 3,500.[26]

A great number or reports from former prisoners
indicate that political opponents of the state suffered
torture ranging from mundane kicks and blows to pain-
ful techniques for extracting information and confessions, including administering electric burns and shocks,
genital mutilation, fingernail plucking, bone crushing,
forcing objects into the anus, and even the rape of
spouses and children before the prisoner. Throughout,
the most commonly used means of torture, undoubtedly
in keeping with the traditions of Iranian history, is reported to have been whipping.

The reports on the widespread use of torture are all
too plausible, to begin with, because of the already noted
similarities of the prison experiences described by released victims. In addition, the Shah himself has claimed
that Savak engaged in interrogation practices involving
torture.

A third source of verification consisted of the periodic
public recantations, in which former dissidents repented
to keep others from going similarly astray. Occasionally
these "reformed terrorists" thanked their captors for the

care accorded their injuries suffered when seeking to escape arrest. The most publicized of such recantations occurred on February 11, 1977. The Iranian press reported:

> Ahmadi [the former Islamic Marxist] joined his wife in thanking the responsible authorities for the kind treatment given to them after their arrest.
>
> We had both jumped off a balcony into the street when we were told the police had come to arrest us. Both of us had broken our arms and our legs and were almost unconscious with pain.
>
> The authorities treated us kindly and we were taken to the hospital. After the preliminary examinations we were taken into surgery.
>
> I hereby wish to publicly thank the officials for their concern and attention. I realize our medical bills must have been at least two million rials.[27]

Suspicions about the use of torture against political prisoners were heightened by the refusal, until recently, of Iranian authorities to allow investigations of the conditions of prisons and prisoners by outside authorities. Occasionally, in the early 1970s, foreign representatives of the International Commission of Jurists or other groups were allowed to send a representative to the trials of political dissidents. When reports critical of these proceedings were forthcoming, such privileges were ended.[28] Following the rather clear signals from the Carter administration, the International Red Cross and a very limited number of foreign journalists were allowed to sit as observers at the trial of a group of "terrorists" in the spring of 1977 and to tour the central Savak prison.[29] Their reports were not sufficiently comprehensive to allow a determination on the continued use of torture. But there were indications that it was used. Finally, if these intimations of the use of torture were not convincing enough, the new regime in Iran has produced the physical evidence. Permanently mangled victims and many of the instruments of torture themselves have eliminated all doubts as to the use of torture by the Shah's regime.

Equally clearly, the judicial process to which dissidents were subject was fundamentally flawed. The accused were unable to prepare a case in their own defense. They were provided a lawyer only shortly before the conduct of the actual trial, without the time or resources to prepare a significant defense. Certain of these "attorneys" who were judged too vigorous in the defense of their clients have been themselves arrested, brought to trial, and imprisoned. In all too many cases persons accused of political dissidence never received a trial at all, but were merely released after a period of detention.

In the most comprehensive review of judicial proceedings ever conducted by an outside observer, Amnesty International's representative concluded that despite certain superficial changes, ". . . the current state of the law in Iran does not in practice represent improvement in the human rights situation. . . ."[30] As a result, in virtually any year during the 1970s, there were as many executions of political opponents carried out by Savak as have been perpetrated by the revolutionary courts of Ayatollah Khomeini.

More broadly considered, it is clear that the distribution of political power in Pahlavi Iran—the intense centralization of financial and political power—was used to effect stringent controls over the frequency and nature of political expression throughout the entire society. Through the dispensation of government advertising, the indirect influence of the security laws, and the direct application of restrictive press laws, the mass media in Iran were restricted to the dissemination of government messages only. All radio and television stations were directly owned by the government and staffed, therefore, by government bureaucrats. Newspapers were privately owned but were intimately involved with the government and no more "independent" than the electronic media. More direct forms of political expression were also controlled by the government. Only one political party was allowed to operate—the National Resurgence party—and membership in the party was seen as a test of one's commitment to Iran's program of royally inspired reforms. The party was split into two wings but both operated well within the ideological confines of the total political system and provided no meaningful political choices. These sectors of the party did not even compete to the extent of fielding different slates in the periodic elections for town and city councils or the national parliament.

Workers were closely controlled as well. Many guilds and worker syndicates existed, but all were organized and supervised by the Ministry of Labor. In effect, the right to strike, as understood in the United States, was denied Iranian workers.

This catalogue of the practice of human rights in Iran under Mohammad Reza Shah Pahlavi could be continued indefinitely. But it should already be clear that no political expression was allowed beyond what the ruling authorities directly sanctioned. A system of differentiated bureaucracies had been developed and operated effectively to control such expression. Finally, there were a variety of security agencies, the most prominent of which was Savak, which dealt vigorously with those who chose to roam outside the explicitly defined guidelines of political activity or expression in Iran.

*   *   *

What is startling, in retrospect, is the speed with which the instruments and procedures of royal rule collapsed. Beginning in 1977, continuing with mounting intensity throughout the year and then erupting in massive anti-regime demonstrations in early 1978 and continuing until the anti-Shah demonstrations which brought more than a million people on the streets of Tehran in orderly and peaceful protests on both December 10 and 11, 1978, the elaborately constructed system collapsed.

Certainly, President Carter's expressions of concern over human rights contributed to the initial expressions of discontent and to the Shah's initially uncertain responses. But too much should not be made of the effect of American human rights policies on the Iranian revolution. That policy undoubtedly had an effect, but in comparison to other, internal dynamics, it was a relatively minor one.

Moreover, as 1977 progressed, the United States gave clear signals that its support for the Shah was, in the words of National Security Advisor Brzezinski "unequivocal and unexceptionable."[31] The decision to sell the Shah his seven AWAC surveillance planes made it clear that the President did not intend to tie arms sales to progress on human rights in Iran. The glowing welcome accorded the Shah on his visit to Washington on November 15, 1977 and the even more glowing tribute to the Shah in Tehran paid by President Carter on New Year's Eve, 1977 were an even more clear message that American interest in progress on human rights was subordinate to maintaining Pahlavi rule.

POSITIVE HUMAN RIGHTS IN IRAN

In addition to civil and political liberties, people should have the right to material, physical, spiritual, and educational well-being. The Shah could boast of dramatic improvements in the standard of living of his people and to improvements in health and education directly due to the increase in oil revenues and a wide variety of reforms which were created and initiated by the regime itself. Beginning with the enunciation of the White Revolution in early 1963, a variety of other reform measures were enacted.[32] Clearly these reforms served to undercut, in some measure, charges by political opponents that the regime was isolated from and disdainful of the Iranian people. In the process the appeal of such critics was reduced while, in turn, the popularity of the Shah and the Empress was enhanced.

Certainly, the execution of the reform laws and in some cases their conceptualization were flawed. Excesses were committed and false expectations raised. In many cases, benefits had been differentially distributed so that the end result was an increase in various measures of inequality in Iran. Certainly, one consequence of the reforms was to increase the social and economic disparities among the people of Iran, not to make for a more homogeneous or egalitarian society.[33] But it remains irrefutably true that the consequence of the reforms has been a decided improvement in overall material well-being.

Educational opportunities were made available to more people (although people in the rural areas and poorest quarters of the cities suffered by comparison with the middle strata). A vast number of new educational institutions at all levels, but particularly post-secondary schools had been established (but their intellectual quality needed strengthening). An ambitious program of government fellowships supported a vast number of students at colleges and universities both within and without Iran (although these are benefits disproportionately available to middle and upper strata families). Every year, a higher percentage of children entered the school system.

Similar improvements can be noted in other areas. The government began a network of new medical centers, dispatching more medical personnel to rural areas, importing physicians from Pakistan, India, and even the Philippines and Korea, and building new medical schools. The electrification of the country, the introduction of new sanitation and water systems, and the modernization of the telephone system were carried out. Various forms of unemployment insurance and poverty grants, day-care centers for the children of the poorest parents, free school lunches, and the training of increased numbers of social workers were introduced. However, as is the case with educational reforms, qualifiers, disclaimers, and serious flaws could be noted for each of these areas. But given problems of execution and design, there is no question but that an ambitious program of government-sponsored, social-welfare measures were launched.

*   *   *

Again, what is startling, retrospectively, is how little support these reforms brought the Shah. While they often did result in gains for the people, no instruments for satisfactorily translating these gains into tangible political support were created. The Rastakhiz party proved disastrously weak in terms of political mobilization. The ulema proved far more successful at mobilizing the people on the bases of their many discontents than did the regime on the basis of its reforms.

HUMAN RIGHTS IN IRAN AND U.S. FOREIGN POLICY

The International Security Assistance and Arms Export Control Act of 1976 commits the United States to

. . . promote respect for and observance of human rights . . . and discourage any practices which are inimical to internationally recognized human rights, and . . . publicly or privately call attention to, and disassociate the United States and any security assistance provided for such country from such practices.[34]

In pursuance of these provisions the United States Department of State was asked to supply information on human rights in Iran to the House of Representatives. Such a report was submitted in late 1976. In its five-page statement, the State Department concluded that continuation of the military assistance program to Iran was in the national interest of the United States. The department argued that Iranian military purchases

are the heart of a program designed to develop a strong Iran. Iran's strength is important to us because of the parallel in Iranian and U.S. national interests found in (1) Iran's defense of its long border with the Soviet Union; (2) the transportation and communications bridge between Europe and Asian countries to the east; (3) Iran's interest in assuming major Persian Gulf security responsibilities previously carried out by the British; (4) Iran's willingness to serve as a reliable source of critical amounts of oil for the United States, Israel, our European allies and Japan; and (5) Iran's activities as a politically stabilizing force throughout that important region from Turkey to the Indian subcontinent.[35]

The United States defined the strategic role of Iran in terms of these vital security functions. Given them, it may very well have been the case that a continuation of security assistance by the United States was appropriate. (It is all too obvious now that the program of flooding Iran with highly sophisticated, destructive, and costly weapons with the acompanying hordes of American civilian and armed forces personnel to train and service the new hardware was not in the interest of either country.)

While the United States security assistance program was deemed appropriate, the Department of State also informed the Congress that

Over the past 2 years, U.S. Government officials have discussed privately with Iranian officials our views about human rights in general and the human rights situation in Iran specifically. These contacts have been guided by our belief that handling this subject privately would be most effective in the Iranian context. To do otherwise would certainly become widely known and would put the matter of human rights in confrontational and self-defeating terms. We have made clear in private converstions our views and laws.[36]

The precise nature of these representations, their intended purposes, the Iranian response, and the consequences, are nowhere reported.

What is at issue here is the fundamental premise on which the Department of State has rested its case in this report: that the strength of Iran would be determined by its possession of military hardware. The United States Department of State does, in fact, possess a more sophisticated view of the bases of Iran's national strength. Its representations to Iranian officials on the issue of human rights in Iran may demonstrate that. Nonetheless, the extremely guarded nature of the State Department's language raises suspicions that such representations may have been aimed more at assuaging the sensibilities of American politicians than altering the nature of Iranian politics.

Traditional Iranian thinking on the question of the bases of national strength itself presents a more differentiated and sophisticated view. In the third century, Ardeshir, the Sassanian, ruled Iran. One of his maxims spoke directly to this issue: "There can be no power without an army, no army without money, no money without agriculture, and no agriculture without justice."[37] And it was 800 years later that the prince of the Caspian region advised his son on the practice of kingship. In the quotation which began this paper he says that the strength of a king rests, fundamentally, on the nature of the relationships among the people and the soldiery and the ruler. The quality of justice is the crucial component which binds the system and produces prosperity.

We see in these views what might be considered the Iranian theory of governance: The perpetuation of rule is based on power which is assured through economic prosperity guaranteed by justice. The issue is whether or not that equation has anything to do with contemporary Iranian political reality. More bluntly, did the availibility of oil revenues to the Shah obviate the fundamentals of the equation? This is a difficult question to answer because of the many current imponderables about the Iranian revolution of 1977. It seems clear that the outcome may have been different. The Shah may have been able to salvage his throne had he responded more vigorously at an earlier stage in the revolution. His response might have been successful had it consisted of a more serious attempt to open the political system to meaningful participation. It might also have been more successful had he used the armed forces more repressively and earlier than he did.

The argument here is that there was nothing inevitable about the revolution of 1977. It need not have occurred when it did. There is every reason to believe that it need not have occurred at all. But it could not have been prevented—although perhaps delayed—without considerably increased attention to human rights in its three dimensions: civil-judicial, economic-social, and political.

In short, the basic Iranian theory of governance does remain valid. Clearly, the prosperity of the realm no longer depends in the first instance on agriculture. And only a relatively small labor force needs to be mobilized to keep the oil flowing out and the petro-dollars flowing in. But Iran is no primitive, desert petroleum exporter. It boasts an economy which has expanded rapidly for two decades and a growing force of industrial skilled labor. It is a country with burgeoning government bureaucracies committed to the provision of a range of complicated political and social services. It fields massive armed forces outfitted with complicated weaponry. It educates tens of thousands of young men and women in and outside Iran. In sum, the prosperity of Iran depends not so much on its oil revenues, but more, to the extent that its oil revenues are translated through a participant, committed labor force into social output.

For a number of years, a fair measure of success in this regard was achieved through a combination of political control, financial largesse, and the initiation of economic and social reform programs. But, as new systems of values infused the society and as traditional systems of authority continued to lose their hold, there was every reason to expect broadened demands for a variety of political freedoms, most especially for genuine political participation.

Rather than meeting those nascent demands, the Shah chose another course in the 1970s: to add severe and increasing repression to traditional modes of social control while strengthening political ties to the United States and infusing Iranian life with many thousands of foreign and in particular American technicians. Both courses served dramatically to lesson the legitimacy of the regime. The Shah came increasingly to be seen as an instrument of American policies and American values. The distance between the regime and the population grew. The revolution of 1977 had many roots, both in the more distant past and in the proximate political present. But a revulsion towards the political repression and the perceived debasement of Iranian culture which resulted from the Shah's modernization programs were two of the primary causes.

This is not to suggest that the Iranian people are yearning for a political system which approximates American democracy. Given the political traditions of Iran and the nature of its indigenous authority systems, from the family to the state, there is very little reason to expect such yearnings. But there is very widespread support, particularly among the educated strata, for greater opportunities for meaningful political participation and civil liberties. Among the entire population there are yearnings for justice, in the form of a judicial system, an economic system, and a social system which represent the highest ideals of indigenous Iranian culture as well as Shi'ite Islam.

The point being reiterated here is that classical Iranian political theory is, in fact, valid in contemporary Iran, irrespective of the changing bases of economic prosperity. Indeed, it may be argued that the theory is now more applicable since the prosperity of the realm depends on the mobilization of a national labor force. The quality of justice in Iran will ultimately determine the future of the present system of organizing the political life of Iran, as has been the case throughout Iranian history.

The ability of the United States to influence the political system of Iran and to foster justice there is now virtually nonexistent. Our commitments to the Shah and the apparently complete support which we accorded the Pahlavi system have eliminated our credibility with all politically active Iranians. The ending of our military assistance programs, the shutting down of most American economic activities in Iran, and the drastic decrease in the American diplomatic presence have left the United States with no means to influence the current Iranian struggle to fashion a new political order. American inefficaciousness stands in dramatic contrast to the situation which pertained under the Shah. Then pressure could have been applied to three principle areas: military, economic, and political. That is, Iran bought massive quantities of arms from the United States and, more tellingly, these required thousands of American military and civilian personnel for operations, training, and maintenance. An important component of the economic relations between the two countries was based on the military sales, but Iran's purchases of industrial technology and nuclear power capability were even more important components of the economic ties. More thousands of Americans lived in Iran to facilitate and foster economic relations. A third major American influence on Iran was political. The United States had the capability of exercising political influence on Iran given the longstanding and pervasive ties at all levels of the political system, the basic common interests, and the military and economic connections between the two states.

In sum, there were an array of means by which American influence towards the development of human rights

in Iran could have been exercized. Moreover, the diversity and depth of the connections between the two countries suggest that these means could have been most
subtle, directed at the appropriate target in a fashion
commensurate with achieving a given end. The issue is
not whether the means to influence Iranian politics existed or what they were, but rather whether or not they
might have been used in the interests of human rights
and what the effects of such use would have been. Given
the extent to which the United States perceived the Shah
as crucial for achieving other aims of American foreign
policy, the Carter administration was wary of incurring
the Imperial wrath by stressing human rights. Such
wrath would surely have been forthcoming from continued attention to human rights in Iran. For the Shah
made his position on human rights explicit, time and
again.

> We are completely in favor of defending human
> rights as long as this is in accordance with the inter-
> ests of the majority. But if this carries us towards the
> law of the jungle and defeat, then it can no longer
> be called human rights.[38]

In short, "human rights" by his definition, were advanced by the policies which the Shah enunciated. They
were, in fact, synonymous with those policies. Of necessity, then, American intervention to advance its own
conception of human rights could have been accomplished only contrary to the designs of the Shah. At least
as often as he stated his position on human rights, he
reiterated his opposition to American efforts to alter his
policies. In the same news conference at which he stated
the conception of human rights which would be tolerated, he also made clear his readiness to buy arms from

other sources should the United States link arms sales to human rights. More broadly, he made it clear in something of a warning, that Iran needed the United States far less than the reverse. He noted that Iran could obtain elsewhere everything it was buying from United States, but ". . . who can replace a friendly Iran for the United States."[39]

The sophistication and subtlety of the Shah in dealing with the United States was demonstrated by his visit to Washington in the fall of 1977. He emerged from his consultations with President Carter as a champion of oil-price stability in the councils of OPEC and, in return, received the promise of a presidential visit to Iran. What was demonstrated, again, was that President Carter, the eighth American president to hold office during the regime of the Shah, valued the many diverse components of the relationship between the United States and Iran too much to risk them on behalf of pressure for human rights. There was, of course, some continued support for human rights emanating from Washington. And the Shah, mindful of his long and beneficial relation with the United States, did respond in some fashion to that pressure. He responded, for example, by ameliorating the fate of political prisoners and terrorists as described above.

What was always evident, however, was that his response was limited to minor cosmetic measures. For the Shah did not, apparently, subscribe to the classical Iranian theory of political rule, at least not in the short run. And, in the interests of achieving other foreign policy goals—principally those detailed by the State Department in justifying continued military sales to Iran—the United States Administration chose not to press for any more fundamental attention to human rights.

Retrospectively, that policy was mistaken. The Shah of

the 1970s was not the same ruler he had been in the 1960s. He had lost touch with his people and their aspirations. He misunderstood the changing political realities of Iran. He underestimated the devastating social effects of his modernization programs and the consequent sense of the devaluation of Iranian culture which those programs represented for Iranians. He also overestimated the support which would be generated by the material improvement which they brought. In many ways, the United States shared his flawed vision. The American failure to press for human rights was partially, then, a reflection of American misperceptions of Iranian realities.

But the failure stemmed from other sources as well. The United States misperceived the extent to which the Shah himself had lost touch with his own people and overestimated his political skills for assuaging their discontent. The Iranians' longings for improvements in human rights were never taken seriously by American policy-makers, who seemed to operate on a quasi-Marxist belief that economic improvement could substitute indefinitely for political participation. Finally, it was clearly the case that remaining in the good graces of the Shah in the short run was more important to American policy than contributing to fundamental changes that might have better assured his rule in the long run.

But the value of such speculations is now clearly limited. For the many means which the United States had for influencing the Iranian political system have been lost. In the foreseeable future the United States will be a spectator rather than an active participant in Iranian affairs. There will undoubtedly be some role for the United States, whatever the form of the post-Shah Iran. But it seems inconceivable that the previous central position of the United States in Iranian life will be regained.

That is not only inconceivable but, given the history of Iran in the 1970s, undesirable for both Iran and the United States. It may have been impossible for the United States to intervene to alter the course of that history. But, more likely, appropriate and focussed intervention to facilitate more meaningful human rights in Iran—civil-judicial, political, and socioeconomic—would have contributed to an Iran very different from that one now struggling to fashion a new political order.

The diverse components of the new regime in Iran remain united in condemning pervasive and serious violations of human rights by the Shah during his 37 year reign. For them, "perpetual atrocities" would more nearly capture that history.

Since his ouster, the Shah has been slightly more conciliatory, acknowledging that some torture did occur under his rule. But this, he claims, was due solely to the excessive zeal—the "human nature"—of his secret police. No official policy, he continues to assert, ever condoned such practices. In any case, he claims to have learned of such torture from foreign reports and to have eliminated torture by mid-1977.

This argumentation over the nature, intensity, and duration of torture and broader human rights violations under Pahlavi rule misses the essential force behind the passion now so manifest in Iran. To understand that passion, one must grasp two points.

First, the Iranian people now believe with virtual unanimity that torture and many other less dramatic violations of human rights were pervasive under the Shah. That belief both contributes to and sustains the near total rejection of the Pahlavi system.

The belief is so deep seated that the new Constitution of the Islamic Republic of Iran states in Principle 38:

Any type of torture to obtain confessions or to acquire information is forbidden. Forcing people to testify, confess, or take an oath is not permitted and such testimony, confession, and taking an oath is null and void.

Second, the people of Iran feel deeply a sense of personal humiliation and cultural debasement. These they attribute to the rule of the Shah and beyond, to the "supreme enemy of mankind"—the United States. The humiliation and debasement are understood to have resulted partially from the Shah's violation of human rights. Thus Principle 39 of the new Constitution, following immediately upon the outlawing of torture states:

Violating the dignity and honor of a person who has been apprehended, detained, arrested or exiled in accordance with the law is forbidden *under any circumstances* and is liable to punishment (italics added).

This principle is one of the very few in the new governing document which cannot be altered by law. It indicates the extent to which Iranians believe they experienced a denigration of their humanness under Pahlavi rule.

Yet another component of that denigration for Iranians can now be understood as the belief that Iranian culture was debased as a result of the Shah's relentless pursuit of "modernization" defined as "westernization" or even "Americanization." Insofar as individuals derive some sense of selfhood from an identification with their culture, the denigration of that culture will result, by extension, in a sense of the denigration of self. That process is generally understood to have occurred in Iran.

In retrospect, then, the Iranian Revolution of 1977-1979 suggests that a fourth component must be added to our conception of human rights—the preservation of the authenticity and integrity of the national culture. For insofar as the Pahlavi system (and it is important to see this process as essentially the responsibility of the entire governing class) came to be understood as debasing Iranian culture, then individual Iranians experienced a humiliation to their sense of selves—surely a fundamental attribute which concern for human rights seeks to preserve.

NOTES

1. Kai Kā'ūs Ibn Iskandar, *The Qābūs Nāma (A Mirror for Princes)* (Reuben Levy, trans.) (London: The Cresset Press, 1951), p. 229.
2. Shahriar Rouhani interview on "Meet the Press," NBC, April 15, 1979.
3. There have been an immense number of accounts of the revolution, either laudatory or analytic. (Totally absent are any which criticize the revolution by supporting the continued rule of the Shah.) Analysis of the revolution can be found in Marvin Zonis, "He Took All the Credit, Now He Gets All the Blame," *The New York Times* (January 14, 1979); Marvin Zonis, "Group Consciousness, Hierarchy, and Stratification in the Iranian Revolution," unpublished paper prepared for a Conference on "Hierarchy and Stratification in the Near and Middle East," ACLS-SSRC Joint Committee on the Near and Middle East, Mt. Kisco, N.Y., 1979; Ervand Abrahamian, "Iran in Revolution: The Opposition Forces," *Middle East Research*

and Information Report, No. 75/76 (April-May, 1979); Ervand Abrahamian. "Political Challenge and Economic Contradictions." *MERIP,* no. 69, n.d.. Longer monographs which analyze the immediate background to the revolution include Robert Graham, *The Illusion of Power* (New York: St. Martin's Press, 1978), and Fred Halliday, *Iran: Dictatorship and Development* (New York: Penguin Books), 1979.

4. Hamid Algar in his "Translator's Forward" to Ali Shari'ati, *On the Sociology of Islam* (Berkeley, California: The Mizan Press, 1979), p. 5. Shari'ati's writings were especially influential with the younger generation of the Iranian intelligentsia who found in his writings a new mode for understanding and expressing their concerns in a fashion faithful to their own sensibilities regarding Iran's cultural and religious heritage rather than abandoning or degrading that cultural authenticity through the wholesale adoption of Western, secular ideas. Of the politically significant figures in the revolution itself, Engineer Mehdi Bazergan, now Prime Minister, and Ayatollah Taleghani, a leading, popular *alim* or Muslim cleric, expressed most vigorously ideas compatible with those of Shari'ati.

5. Reza Earaheni has published a number of vivid accounts of his incarceration and torture as well as a volume (in English) of his prison poems. See, for example, his *God's Shadow* (Bloomington, Indiana: Indiana University Press, 1976) which contains forty-one such poems as well as a lengthy prose account of his prison experiences. See also his article, "Terror in Iran," in *The New York Review* (October 28, 1976), pp. 21-25 and "The Shah's Torture Chambers," in *Penthouse* (February, 1977), pp. 90-91, 128-130 and *The Crowned Cannibals, Writings on Repression in Iran* (New York: Vintage Books, 1977).

6. For additional information on Iranian students in the United States and Iranian higher education, see C.K. Eicher, A.J. Lewis, A.L. Morton, and M. Zonis, *An Analysis*

of US-Iranian Cooperation in Higher Education (Washington, D.C.: Overseas Liaison Committee, American Council on Education, 1976).

7. See, for example, *Resistance—Quarterly English Defense Publication of the Iranian Students' Association in the United States* and *The Iranian People's Struggle,* the bulletin of the Iranian National Front.

8. See, for example, *Report by Amnesty International on Political Prisoners in Iran* (August 12, 1976), and the annual report on international violations of human rights by Amnesty International (Fall, 1976). Also see Amnesty International, *Iran* (November, 1976). One of the most powerful statements on the subject was the testimony of an Amnesty International representative, Brian Wrobel, who visited Iran in April, 1977, and subsequently testified, February 28, 1978, before the Subcommittee on International Organizations of the Committee on International Relations, The House of Representatives. His testimony was reported in *The New York Times* (March 1, 1978) and published in *The Congressional Record* as well as in a 60-page document by Amnesty International.

9. William J. Butler and Georges Levasseur, *Human Rights and the Legal System in Iran* (Geneva: International Commission of Jurists, May, 1976).

10. *Human Rights and U.S. Policy: Argentina, Haiti, Indonesia, Iran, Peru, and The Phillipines,* Reports submitted to the Committee on International Relations, U.S. House of Representatives, by the Department of State, December 31, 1976.

11. *Human Rights in Iran,* Hearings before the Subcommittee on International Organizations of the Committee on International Relations of the U.S. House of Representatives, August 3 and September 8, 1976. See also the reference to Wrobel above.

12. For a more comprehensive analysis of U.S.-Iranian relations in the 1950s and 1960s, see this author's *The Political Elite Of Iran* (Princeton: Princeton University Press, 1971); Sharam Chubin and Sepehr Zabih, *The Foreign*

Relations of Iran—A Developing State in Zone of Great Power Conflict (Berkeley: University of California Press, 1974); James A. Bill, *The Politics of Iran* (Columbus: Charles E. Merrill, 1972); and Rouhollah K. Ramazani, *The Foreign Policy of Iran* (Charlottesville: University of Virginia Press, 1975).

13. *U.S. Military Sales to Iran.* A Staff Report to the Subcommittee on Foreign Assistance of the Committee on Foreign Relations, U.S. Senate, July, 1976.

14. *Kayhan,* Weekly International Edition (February 12, 1977), pp. 1,3.

15. Ibid.

16. Mīrzā Alī, Deputy Minister of Foreign Affairs to the British Ambassador, Mr. McNeill, dated January 6, 1838 from Correspondences Relating to Persia and Afghanistan, London, 1839, p. 102, as quoted by A.K.S. Lambton, "Persian Society Under the Qajars," *Royal Central Asian Society Journal,* Vol. XLVIII, vol. 4, no. 1, part II, p. 128.

17. For example, one foreign observer described how Agha Mohammed Khan initiated the new Qajar dynasty:

    The city of Kerman was treated with inconceivable cruelty. Not only were its women handed over to the soldiery who were encouraged to rape and murder, but the Kajar victor ordered that twenty thousand pairs of eyes should be presented to him. These he carefully counted and then he remarked to the officer charged with the atrocious task, "Had one pair been wanting, yours would have been taken." Thus almost the entire male population was blinded and their women were handed over to the soldiery as slaves. In order to commemorate the capture of Lutf Ali Khan [his chief rival] in a suitable manner, Agha Mohammad ordered six hundred prisoners to be decapitated. Their skulls were then carried to Bam by three hundred other prisoners who were then also killed, and a pyramid of skulls was erected on the spot where Lutf Ali Khan was taken [in 1794]. This pyramid was seen by Pottinger in 1810. Kerman never recovered.

Sir Percy Sykes, *A History of Persia* (London: Macmillan and Company, 1963 [1915]), Vol. I, p. 288.

18. An Englishman was hired by one such landowner following World War I to manage his estate of some 96 villages covering 500 square miles. (This was not a particularly large holding, many Iranian grandees boasting hundreds of villages and some, more than five hundred. Reza Shah himself ended his life personally owning over two thousand villages in the richest agricultural region of Iran.) The Englishman makes clear how the landowner, Sardar Akram, was the sole dispenser of "justice," with physical punishments—in particular the bastinado, or the flaying of the soles of the feet—being widely used. See F.A.C. Forbes-Leith, *Checkmate, Fighting Tradition in Central Persia* (London: George C. Harrap and Company, Ltd., n.d.).

19. Mr. Cunningham Greene in a private letter to Lord Kimberly, July 21, 1894, as quoted by Rose Greaves, "British Policy in Persia, 1892-1903," *Journal of the British School of Oriental and African Studies*, Vol. 28, 1965, p. 44.

20. Lt. Colonel Stuart, *Journey of a Residence in Northern Persia* (London, 1854), p. 235.

21. Robert A. McDaniel, *The Shushter Mission and The Persian Constitutional Revolution* (Minneapolis: Bibliotheca Islamica, 1974), p. 202.

22. For an excellent essay on the development of human rights in the West, see Richard P. Claude, "The Classical Model Of Human Rights Development," in Richard P. Claude, ed., *Comparative Human Rights* (Baltimore: The Johns Hopkins University Press, 1976), pp. 6-50.

23. It is a striking fact of Iranian life that the efflorescences of cruelty which so frequently characterize Iranian history are matched by equal demonstrations of gentleness. Thus, the height of the Constitutional Revolution, from December 1905, to the granting of the document in August, 1906, was notable for its total absence of bloodshed.

24. For a list of many of these trials, see William J. Butler, op, cit., passim.

25. The same organization lists the number of political prisoners in the U.S.S.R. as 6000!

26. *Human Rights in Iran,* op. cit., p. 25.

27. "Recruitment to Terrorism—How Ringleaders Exploit the Innocent," *Kayhan International* (February 12, 1977), pp. 4-5.

28. For a typical critical account, see "Report of Mr. Terry Mignon, Attorney at Law in Finance to the World Federation of Human Rights—July 6, 1971," mimeographed.

29. For a report of one of these visits, see Richard T. Sale, "SAVAK: A Feared and Pervasive Force," *The Washington Post* (May 9, 1977), pp. 1, A7.

30. Brian Wrobel, op. cit., p. 3.

31. As related by Zbigniew Brzezinski to the author, November 15, 1978.

32. There are a considerable number of recent works which discuss various aspects of these reforms. For a start there is the Shah's own view of these processes. See Mohammad Reza Shah Pahlavi, *The White Revolution of Iran,* Tehran: Kayhan Press, n.d.

33. For some impressive studies on the changing nature of inequality in Iran, see Farhad Mehran, "Income Distribution in Iran, The Statistics of Inequality," Working Paper, *Income Distribution and Employment Program* (Geneva: International Labor Office, October, 1975); M. H. Pesaran, "Income Distribution Trends in Rural and Urban Iran," Paper prepared for a Conference, "The Social Sciences and Problems of Development—Iran, June 1-4, 1974; M.H. Pesaran, "Income Distribution and Its Major Determinants in Iran," Paper prepared for "Aspen-Persepolis Symposium—Iran: Past, Present, and Future, September 15-19, 1975; Jiri Skolka and Michel Garzuel, "Changes in Economic Distribution, Employment, and Structure of the Economy: A Case Study of Iran," Working Paper, *Income Distribution and Employment Program* (Geneva: In-

ternational Labor Office, September, 1976); and George E. Wright, Jr., *Regional Inequality in the Economic Development of Iran, 1962-1970,* Unpub. Ph.D. Dissertation, The University of Michigan, 1977.

34. Text of Section 502B (c) from the Act as reproduced in Committee on International Relations, U.S. House of Representatives, *Human Rights and U.S. Policy: Argentina, Haiti, Indonesia, Iran, Peru, and The Philippines,* Reports submitted by the Department of State, December 31, 1976, p. 37. It must be added that the Act specifies no automatic cut-off of U.S. assistance in the event of a finding of human rights violations.

35. Ibid., p. 22.

36. Ibid., p. 21.

37. Sykes, op. cit., Vol. I, p. 397.

38. Mohammad Reza Shah Pahlavi, Shahanshah, at a news conference as reported by *Kayhan International Weekly* (June 25, 1977), p. 1.

39. Ibid.

Korea, Human Rights and United States Foreign Policy

DONALD L. RANARD

INTRODUCTION

Viewed from either side, the single most controversial issue confronting relations between the United States and Korea for three-quarters of a century has been human rights. In its earliest manifestation, the problem largely related to self-determination as China, Russia, and Japan each maneuvered in turn to control and influence Korean affairs. In November, 1895 Secretary of State Olney instructed his envoy in Seoul to "Confine yourself strictly [to] protection of American citizens and interests, . . . You have no concern in internal affairs."[1]

Some 80 years later, Secretary of State Kissinger was instructing the American ambassador in Seoul to "get off the backs" of the South Korean government as an authoritarian South Korean president denied his countrymen their basic human rights. Yet, in the meanwhile, the United States had fought a bloody war in Korea and, through massive military and economic aid, had become deeply involved on the peninsula in an effort to establish a "showcase of democracy" south of the Demilitarized Zone. Moreover, internationally the United States had taken the leadership in establishing the United Nations, the charter of which, as well as the provisions of the Universal Declaration of Human Rights, had required

177

of its membership a pledge to observe, respect, and promote human rights and fundamental freedoms.

What do we mean when we refer to the deprivations of human rights in Korea? Why has the United States avoided for so long its responsibilities for advancing the cause of human rights in a country it had defended with its blood and treasure? Is there a legitimate role for human rights in the context of national security considerations that the United States faces on the Korean peninsula?

A DISMAL RECORD BEGINS

In South Korea human rights were first denied when Syngman Rhee moved vigorously following the end of World War II to establish himself as undisputed leader below the 38th parallel. Rhee jailed and "eliminated" his competitors, controlled or closed the press, forced his measures through the National Assembly (sometimes locking it up until it capitulated), capriciously interpreted the Constitution, rigged national elections and more than once corrupted the balloting.

Then, as now, the Department of State's rationale for tolerating violations of human rights in South Korea was national security. Less than two years after the Republic of Korea was established in 1948 and Rhee installed as president, an aggressive and cruel regime to the north had invaded the south. Three years later fighting ceased with an armistice agreement, which both sides, first at Geneva and then subsequently in the United Nations, were unable to supplant with permanent arrangements for settling the Korean question.

For the next decade, as an aging Rhee tightened the reins of government, the memories of the war with its economic devastation and physical suffering were so real as to downgrade the priority of human rights. Moreover, Rhee had considerable popular appeal. He was an acknowledged patriot who had kept alive aspirations for Korean independence during the Japanese occupation; his record against the Japanese, a *sine qua non* of Korea politics, was second to none. In this situation, Koreans were prepared to wait, while watching the north, internal developments, and the reaction of the United States to both. While Washington tolerated Rhee's repressive acts, Koreans were unprepared to challenge their government. The tolerance of the United States briefly lapsed following the national elections of March 1960. The rigging of the electoral process and the accompanying torture of political and student dissidents was so blatant that the United States government was impelled to speak out publicly. After the ensuing April revolution, led by high school and college students, Rhee fell from power.

In assessing Rhee's abuses, certain factors are worth emphasis because they explain Washington's reactions to and tolerance of events under Rhee as they anticipate and highlight subsequent deprivations by President Park Chung-hee. First, the threat from the north was real, immediate, and fresh in mind. The north was militarily strong, and the recipient of aid and attention from a Sino-Soviet bloc not yet divided by unbridgeable rifts. Second, the United States was still deeply preoccupied in Asia by the "loss of China," and disturbed by Soviet intentions over Berlin and the development of communism on its door-step in Latin America. And finally, no matter how egregious Rhee's violations, the Constitution of 1948 had established the Republic of Korea as a legal government under laws which promoted democratic institutions and respect for human rights. While a police-state mentality flourished, the excesses of the Korean Central Intelligence Agency, with stations throughout Korea, and indeed in many of the world capitals, were yet unknown. Whatever may be said of the violations of rights that may have been made in the period which followed Rhee, at least it was not undemocratic. If Chang Myun's government was ineffective, as charged by those who seek to justify the 1961 coup, he nevertheless was dedicated to human rights and moral values. Regrettably he was removed by a military junta, and on July 3, 1961, Major-General Park Chung-hee became chairman of the newly formed Supreme Council for National Reconstruction, and with him began a record of violations of human rights worse than that of any government with which the United States maintains bilateral defense treaty alliances.

Human Rights at their Nadir

So commonplace has become the awareness of the violations in Park's Korea that long-since forgotten is how it all began. In fact, the first assault began with General Park's illegal ascent to power. In May 1961, Park, a handful of disgruntled colonels and 3500 troops (out of a military service of 600,000) struck against a government generally acknowledged as the first freely elected in Korea. In Seoul, Prime Minister Chang Myun, deceived by his Army Chief of Staff, hesitated. Washington, tied up by bureaucratic indecisions during President Kennedy's visit to Canada, waited cautiously for further developments. During this time, the coup was consolidated and the march toward one-man rule began.

In the years that followed, an insecure and inexperienced military junta first overreacted with draconian measures, but then gradually relaxed. The economy improved, aided considerably by Korean foreign-exchange earnings from Vietnam. Park was narrowly elected to office in the corrupted elections of 1963 and 1967. In 1969, with further tenure prohibited by constitutional limitation, he rammed through a constitutional amendment providing for a third term. The *Pueblo* affair and the Blue House raid (1968) had again reminded the populace of the provocative threat from the north and this Park continued to manipulate. For the opposition, as indeed for Koreans at large, the only hope was the election of 1971. But it proved to be otherwise. The period beginning with the election of 1971 in fact marks the nadir of representative government in South Korea. Over the past eight years Park has violated human rights far more than did Syngman Rhee and with less cause. For one thing, he corrupted the 1971 national election, in which he defeated Kim Tae-chung by close to a million votes. Notwithstanding Park's heavy-handed manipulation of the media and the all-out engagement of his bureaucratic apparatus, Kim managed to poll 46 percent of the vote, thus leading many to conclude he would have won in a free and fair contest. (Park has since curbed the electoral process for president. As a result, in mid-1978, he was again elected in what a leading American congressmen termed "a Soviet-styled uncontested election.")

In the fall of 1972, in the middle of what he had promised would be his last term in office, Park Chung-hee declared martial law, abandoned the constitution, dismissed the national assembly, closed the universities, censored the press, and while the country was still under military rule, brought in a so-called "revitalizing" (*Yushin*) constitution. While the country was under martial law, Park was elected for six years without limitation on tenure by the National Conference for Unification, which he chaired. To further broaden his control of the state, the constitution was changed to allow him to appoint the prime minister, one third of the members of the new national assembly, the 16 members of the supreme court, as well as the constitution committee which sat to judge the constitutionality of laws, impeachment, and dissolution of a political party.

To leave no doubt as to who was in charge, Article 53 was written into the constitution. It provided that in times of national emergency, the president was empowered "to take necessary emergency measures in the whole range of State affairs, including internal affairs, foreign affairs, national defense, economic, financial and judicial affairs." The president was to be the sole judge of the nature of emergency measures, their need, and their duration; there was no requirement for consent of the assembly, moreover, nor were such measures "subject to judicial deliberations thereon."

And what of the rights and guarantees of freedom defined in the previous constitution? They were similarly peremptorily treated: the president was given "the power to take emergency measures which temporarily suspend the freedom and rights of the people." Whereas, citizen liberties and rights had previously been restricted by law only as required for the maintenance of order and public welfare, the revised law allowed far greater latitude by the president. In instance after instance, rights and liberties were thus limited, as for example, "no citizen shall be subject to restriction of freedom of speech and press, or freedom of assembly and association, *except as provided by law.* . . ." It was with this in mind that William J. Butler, then Vice President of the American Association for the International Commission of Jurists, following a visit to Seoul in mid-1974 on behalf of Amnesty International, characterized the Korean document as "one of the most authoritarian instruments presently known in the annals of national constitutions, including the constitutions of communist nations."[2]

Park authorized kidnappings and other acts of terrorism, both at home and abroad. Of these, by far the most flagrant (although not as grandiose as the 1967 kidnapping of Korean students in Germany) was the kidnapping in Tokyo in early August 1973 of Kim Taechung. Kim was out of Korea when Park made his "Constitutional coup" in late 1972. Fearing for his safety, Kim remained abroad attempting in both the United States and Japan to alert the press and public to the increasing danger to personal freedoms under Park's rule. The Korean C.I.A. put him under surveillance, harassed his activities, and intimidated his followers. Subsequently, they kidnapped him from his hotel in Tokyo.[3] After several years in jail on trumped-up charges of having plotted against the state (he aptly called Park a "generalissimo") Kim was released in December 1978 but placed under virtual house arrest. The human rights issues involved? Just about every article in the Universal Declaration as well as the International Covenant on Civil and Political Rights guaranteeing the security of the person.

In December 1973 Park was faced with a growing demand for reinstatement of the earlier constitutional guarantees. When Park's warnings failed to stop petitions for redress the government responded in early January 1974 with Emergency Measures No. 1 and No. 2, and later in April with measure No. 4. Essentially, Emergency Measure No. 1 made it a crime to advocate repeal of the constitution, subject to imprisonment up to 15 years. Emergency Measure No. 2 substituted martial law tribunals for civilian courts in cases of so-called crimes committed under the emergency. Emergency Measure No. 4 prohibited political activity in connection with or support of a certain student organization alleged to be friendly to the north. So sweeping was this measure that, taken literally, it could mean the death penalty for students who cut classes or engaged in political activities, even including sit-ins. Even though these measures were revoked the following year, they were followed by one equally repressive, Emergency Measure No. 9, which still is in effect. How many people were caught up in these regulations is open to question. According to the South Korean government, which has invariably minimized such accounts, some 1024 people were detained, 253 referred for prosecution, 750 released and 55 convicted under Emergency Measure No. 4. Another 36 people were sentenced under Emergency Measure No. 1.[4]

Cruel, inhumane and degrading treatment or punishment has long been government's method in Korea for obtaining information from people under suspicion as well as for intimidating them. This has been applied to people of influence and prominence who simply have opposed President Park politically as well as to those charged with major crimes of aiding the north or allegedly plotting to overthrow the government. While the Department of State has carefully avoided condemning the South Korean government, a careful reading of testimony by the Department before Congress easily leads to the conclusion that the charges are valid.[5]

Easily the most damaging case concerns the execution in April 1975 of eight members of the Peoples Revolutionary party (PRP), an illegal organization allegedly allied to North Korea and claimed to have plotted the overthrow of the South Korean government. In a highly controversial case in 1964, 47 alleged members of the PRP were charged with subversion, but cases against 34 were dismissed due to insufficient evidence (so flimsy were the grounds that three public prosecutors resigned rather than charge the defendants). The balance received light or suspended sentences. A decade later the government dusted off the files and once again fabricated a case against the PRP, this time not containing its fury until eight alleged members were hanged in April 1975. An amnesty mission visiting Seoul at that time reported that all the accused admitted the charges under torture. They were executed in spite of the fact that the evidence presented fell short of proof that the defendants were in fact involved in the alleged conspiracy. In addition, the defendants were not allowed to present defense witnesses, and prosecution witnesses were called even though defense lawyers were not present. Nor were the defense lawyers allowed to cross examine prosecution witnesses.[6]

Charges of violation of freedom of thought, of religion, of opinion, and of assembly have not been uncommon in modern Korea, but the government reactions to the Samil Declaration of 1976 probably best illustrate the status of these freedoms in South Korea. On March 1, 1976 a group of leading Christian and political leaders gathered in Seoul's Myungdong Cathedral where they signed and issued a "Patriotic Declaration of Democracy" calling for an end to the repressive emergency measures, restoration of basic human rights, and an independent legislature and judiciary. As a result of what the foreign press regarded as a "moderate, even vapid, declaration," 18 were quickly arrested and charged with provoking a popular uprising. Included were Kim Tae-chung; 79-year-old ex-president Yun Po-sun; former Foreign Minister, Chung Il-hyun (73) and his lawyer wife Yi Tae-young, and Hahn Suk-hon (76), a well-known Quaker dissident whose resistence to repression began against the Japanese more than a half century earlier.

In August 1976 they were sentenced to between five and eight years, the more prominent receiving the heavier sentences. On appeal, sentences were reduced, and finally in March 1977 convictions were upheld by the Supreme Court. Sentences were suspended for nine including Yun Po-sun, Chung Il-hyun and his wife and Hahn. Kim Tae-chung was finally released in December 1978 at which time the government also reduced the life sentence of Kim Chi-ha, the country's leading poet to 20 years. Park Chung-hee also has destroyed the freedom of the press. He did this by first forcing South Korea's most prestigious newspaper, the *Tonga-Ilbo* to hire management and a reportorial staff more sympathetic to the regime.[7] Perhaps the best indication of how hobbled the Korean press is today is seen in its obsequious treatment of the KCIA-Park Tong-sun bribery scandal—easily the biggest news story affecting relations with the United States of the seventies. For months the press was completely silent; then it was allowed to refer to the scandal but without reference to any link to President Park or the Blue House role, both of which were directly implicated in congressional hearings of 1977 and 1978.

The government has been equally effective in its manipulation of the courts. In the trial of the alleged members of the PRP, as well as those of the 18 Samil dissidents, and the earlier trials of Kim Tae-chung and Kim Chi-ha, law has been subordinated to the command of dictatorial rule.

Basic economic rights related to conditions of work, fair wages, the right to strike, and collective bargaining have been denied. Especially is this true in textiles which comprise the country's largest industry. Here, a labor force of 700,000 works as much as 10 hours a day, six days a week at subsistence wages, with many averaging $60 to $70 monthly. Efforts by textile workers to organize and strike for better working conditions have met with beatings, arrest, and dismissal. Thus while the South Korean government, and indeed the State Department, is quick to point to World Bank statistics hailing a "relatively egalitarian pattern of income distribution," it is well to note the cost in human dignity.

U.S. POLICY

Over the past 25 years the United States has wanted to avoid conflict in Korea. For nowhere else in the world do the superpowers, nuclear-armed, confront each other as they do across the peninsula's 38th parallel. The north is backed by both the Soviet Union and China, with whom it has defense alliances; and the South is similarly fortified by the United States. Conflict could escalate into nuclear war, and this horrible possibility is ever in the minds of decision-makers in the United States, as well as in Moscow and Peking. For both the Soviet Union and China, war on the peninsula, unlike Vietnam, would not allow a spectator role. Both not only have common boundaries with the north, but more importantly uncertain borders with each other. Conflict in Korea could serve to distract the attention of the one, while enticing the other to military resolution of their border disputes. And so it is that whenever major incidents have occurred since the late sixties—the Pueblo seizure in 1968 or the DMZ tree-cutting incident of August 1976—both the Soviet Union and China have reacted cautiously. For example, in 1968 the evidence is that China told Kim Il-Sung to refrain from starting any incidents, and in 1976, as tempers flared in Panmunjon, both Moscow and Peking kept quiet in an obvious effort to keep Kim Il-Sung from miscalculating the extent to which they might be prepared to back his provocation.[8]

To achieve its objective, Washington has maintained, at great financial cost, adherence to the defense commitment and stationing of sizeable military forces (still over 30,000) on the peninsula since the end of the Korean war. It has also provided military and economic assistance totaling $13 billion since 1945. This policy has achieved some semblance of stability along the DMZ while enabling the South Korean economy to move forward dramatically. But it has also sustained the most repressive government of any in the so-called "free world."

Given the circumstances on the peninsula and in northeast Asia during the past two decades, as well as the Sino-Soviet split, could American policy have been otherwise? Was it possible to obtain the objective implied in the oft-quoted Acheson note to the korean government in 1950: "U.S. aid, both military and economic, to the Republic of Korea has been predicated upon the existence and growth of democratic institutions within the Republic"? Could the U.S. have acted otherwise?

REALITIES AND MYTHS

Serving to thwart the initiative of the United States to promote Korean democracy have been a series of concerns—many genuine yet others more fancied than real. Of these, none has had greater impact on the Korean question than the threat from the North.

The Threat

Since 1950 Kim Il-Sung has wanted to unify Korea under his leadership. He launched a war of aggression in 1950, carried out a campaign of terrorism thereafter, attempted to assassinate Park in 1968, and subsequently turned to diplomacy in bilateral talks as well as at the UN and internationally. For the most part, Kim's efforts have met with failure even though he has a formidable army, which, according to more recent intelligence estimates is between 560-600,000 ground troops; an air force of 45,000 with some 655 combat aircraft (320 of which are super-annuated MIG 15-17's, inferior to anything in the South Korean inventory); and a small navy which relies heavily on coastal patrol craft, including some 20 fast missile-firing attack boats whose mission is harassment of South Korean fishing vessels as well as infiltration of agents into the South. In addition, the north is said to have 15 small submarines, whose role presumably is minelaying and interruption of resupply to the south in time of war. Estimates of the fighting capacity of this machine vary. Undoubtedly highly disciplined and tough on the ground and reported to be backed up by heavier firepower than the south, the north is weaker in modern tactics of warfare (it has not been in combat since 1953). Military intelligence estimates, while always emphasizing the numerical advantage of the north in the air, downgrade pilot training, time in the air, and logistics (petroleum, especially). Moreover, the north has nothing in the air to compete with the south's vaunted F-4's (55 on hand, about 18 to follow), as well as its growing force of F 5E/F's (about 111 on hand, with 35 on order).[9]

Arrayed against this force is a strong South Korean Army roughly comparable in numbers (about 560,000) and superior in training and recent field experience (in Vietnam), and access to the modern technology of the West. In addition, there are the United States ground forces in Korea. It seems fair to conclude that, with or without American strength, North Korea could be contained unless the Chinese or the Soviets engage their forces, a possibility considered highly unlikely by most military and political observers. In fact, this is an eventuality made even more remote by the opening of diplomatic relations between the United States and China which is now considered to exercise more influence in Pyongyang than the Soviet Union.

Economic Disparities

The north's recent economic performance has reduced the credibility of its strategic threat.[10] Hurt badly by the oil crunch of 1973, which occurred in the midst of large industrial development, North Korea accumulated a trade deficit of about $2.5 billion by mid-1978 (which resulted in a sizeable default to Japan, possibly as high as $350 million, as well as to Sweden and Finland). North Korea was known to be in serious difficulty in the fall of 1975. The north also lacks advanced technology and scientific manpower, which serve to raise further questions about the north's warmaking capacity, and especially so when contrasted to the south, which has an increasing number of trained scientists and engineers.

Military Expenditures

There are other factors that must serve to restrict Kim Il-Sung's ambitions and to cast doubt on alarmist estimates of his potential harm. Since 1971 the United

States has financed a large-scale modernization of the South Korean armed forces. Through FY 1980 approximately $725 million will have been provided by the United States in additional Foreign Military Sales financing as part of a five-year $2 billion package (which included a grant of $800 million in military equipment) to compensate South Korea for the withdrawal of American ground forces. To finance its expanded "Force Improvement," Korea had already inaugurated military expenditures in 1976 of $4 to 5 billion above its regular defense budget.[11]

South Korea has increased its own military expenditures from $542 million in 1973 to $3.25 billion in 1979 at the same time Kim Il-Sung's economy was in trouble and he was being forced to give more attention to civilian demands (in 1977 North Korea's defense expenditures were estimated at $1.03 billion). Not only was South Korea's economy outpacing that of the north, (whose population of 17 million is roughly one-half the size of the South) so also were her imports of military goods. In the ten-year period between 1967 and 1976, the south imported two-and-one-half times the dollar value of military hardware entering the north: $3.4 billion against $1.4 billion (constant dollars). The gap between the GNP of both countries was even greater: $31.5 billion for the south, $9.8 billion for the north in 1977. And the differential by 1978 was probably greater as the south reached almost $46 billion.[12]

Kim's Succession

While observers of events in North Korea are always intrigued with the apparent problem of Kim Il-Sung's succession, little authoritative information is available on who might succeed him. There have been numerous reports from Pyongyang regarding Kim's choice of Chong-il (his son by his first wife) as his successor. Reportedly this has resulted in a power struggle involving Kim, his present wife, his younger brother Kim Young-ju (who earlier appeared to be the most likely to succeed Kim), and the military.[13] This issue, developing at about the same time as changes in the top leadership of the Korean Workers party, leads to speculation concerning their cumulative impact on peninsular security. There are those who believe that an aging and ill Kim must make his move to unify Korea before the widening gap in relative economic performance rules this out completely. Others emphasize however that Kim has been prudent, especially when dealing with such dangerous incidents as the seizure of the *Pueblo* in 1968. He also backed off in the north-west island dispute of 1973 as well as during the August 1976 tree-cutting incident, and in mid-July 1977 gave every indication he did not intend to allow the helicopter shoot-down to escalate into armed confrontation. While internal developments in North Korea are bound to have an impact on peninsular affairs over the long run, there certainly are no danger signals; in fact there is as much reason to believe the impact will be favorable. This is the conclusion of at least one observer, who believes that "the changing membership of high echelon leadership groups and revised cadres policies suggest that the DPRK may opt" for following the more relaxed policies of other communist countries.[14] In this regard China's move toward normalization of relations with the West cannot but be helpful.

The Sino-Soviet Implication

Whatever their varying estimates of the threat, practically all intelligence analysts and scholars are agreed on one forecast: Neither the Soviet Union nor China sees gain in any recurrence of North Korean armed aggression. Not only would it seriously complicate their bilateral relations, but it would also obstruct the process of détente, economic as well as political, with the United States and Japan. And without such support, Kim Il-Sung for the foreseeable future and probably for the remainder of his lifetime must seek other ways, most likely peaceful and diplomatic, to achieve his objectives.

The Japanese Connection

"Korea is a dagger pointed at the heart of Japan" is the most quoted political briefer's introduction to the Japanese connection. From this invariably follows the assessment that the United States cannot afford the loss of Japan and her tremendous economy and industrial development to the Soviets and communism. The implication? If South Korea goes communist, Japan's security would be threatened. Japan would then either turn right toward remilitarization and nuclear arms or left towards communism. Accordingly, the rationale goes, the United States cannot risk human rights initiatives that might raise tensions in the south, invite aggression by the north, and destabilize East Asia.

This reasoning contains at least two flaws. First, no matter how sizeable the opposition to Park in the south, there is unanimous distrust of the north and its "great father leader" Kim Il-Sung. This repugnance for communism is as true of the Samil dissidents as it is of Park's cabinet ministers. The likelihood of a communist takeover of Korea by any means short of war is practically nil, and as noted earlier, even by military aggression the north's chances of victory are especially slim. As put by Professor Reischauer: "South Korea is no South Vietnam. Its people are solidly unified against the Communist North, still remembering its ruthlessness and cruelty when it overran most of the South during the Korean War. They have twice the population of the North, and a more vigorous economy. South Korea most certainly will not crumble, no matter how hard the North Korea dictator Kim Il-Sung may huff and puff."[15] Much of this assessment is agreed to by American intelligence, including those who nevertheless continue to raise the spectre of a communist peninsula to justify increased military assistance to South Korea.

The second oversimplification concerns the Korean-Japanese relationship. Despite, one might even say because of, its 35-year occupation of Korea, as well as its almost omnipotent economic power in Asia, Japan is in effect a hostage to Korean, and for that matter, regional political sensitivities. As a result, Japan is subject to considerable political pressure from South Korea regarding security issues. Mindful of the ease with which the South Korean government can stage an anti-Japanese demonstration, Japan is publicly circumspect and goes along with Korean assessments. Privately, however, its views are frequently more open-minded.

Obviously Korea is important to Japan, politically, economically, and strategically, but there actually is no unanimity of thought in Japan regarding the degree of importance. In fact, there is strong sentiment in Japan, especially in socialist, intellectual and press circles against the continued presence of United States military forces on the Korean peninsula. In the past Japan was prepared to reiterate, albeit under persuasion from the United States, that South Korea's security was "essential" to that of Japan, a position announced initially in the Nixon-Sato Joint Communique of November 21, 1969. More recently, during Prime Minister Takeo Fukuda's visit to Washington in March 1977 the relationship between Korea's security and that of Japan was described in the communique that followed as "important,"[16] a decided downgrading apparently sought by the Japanese side. (This lesser appraisal of the relationship has been stated by the Japanese side on other occasions.) Whether this reflected increasing division of thought in Japan on Korea, or possibly acknowledgment of the inevitability that the United States might cut its troops in Korea, is perhaps secondary. What is fundamental is that not all Japanese view Korea's security as vital to Japan. This assessment may be confirmed by the fact that the Japanese have never volunteered to house addican forces.

Even if the communists did take over the whole Korean peninsula, would Japan succumb and thus turn the balance of power in the Pacific against American security? Given the vitality of Japan's open society, the strength of her democratic experience, the limited communist appeal at the polls, and perhaps most of all, the vigor of her free enterprise economy, there is reason for great skepticism about the likelihood of a communist Japan. Rather, argues Reischauer, the Japanese would adjust to a united communist Korea, if it came about without the loss of American force and credibility. This would be a relatively easy matter for the Japanese to adjust to. A broad sea border would still exist between them and Korea, and they are already used to having the majority of their neighboring people under communist rule.[17]

Yet, given her stake in Korea and certainly her business investments, Japan quite naturally worries about stability on the peninsula, as well as in Asia generally. But what she is mainly concerned about is the commitment of the United States to the defense of a free Asia (differentiated only as concerns communism) and not the size of its military forces. As I have said, a planned and orderly withdrawal of American ground forces from Korea would not necessarily be seen by Japan as injurious to her own security. In fact, if the United States kept Japan completely informed, Japan might even see this as leading eventually to some sort of four-power security pact guaranteeing the independence and neutrality of the peninsula.

South Korea's Internal Stability

American initiatives to ensure human rights are prevented, as well, by the political rivalry and factionalism that arose after Park Chung-hee seized the government, and it has continued to bedevil the political opposition. To be sure, this has been aided and abetted by an affluent and devious government that has not only bought votes in the United States Congress and the Japanese Diet, but has also bought out certain leading members of the opposition in Korea. The result has been the inability of the opposition to consolidate behind a candidate who could stand solidly against Park. In addition, the KCIA would not allow any opposition candidate, no matter how strongly supported, to win an election. In fact, as the electorate went to the polls in 1971, Park's supporters were making known that a vote for Kim was a wasted ballot; the military would not let him rule if elected. This circumstance led some American policy-makers to conclude that Park was the only man who could lead Korea. The fact that some five million Koreans did not share this estimate in 1971 got lost in the myth that Park and the military promoted. (A refined variation of this theme was circulated by the Korean

Embassy in Washington as it reacted to increasing criticism of Park from the American press and public: "Efforts to get rid of Park could be counter-productive. He might well be succeeded by someone far more repressive.")

The policy makers also were inclined to tolerate Park because they thought that initiatives taken against him could lead to internal instability, violence, and uncertain change of leadership. This concern was not without some substance. Forceful warnings by the State Department to Syngman Rhee, both in Washington and Seoul, regarding his flagrantly undemocratic conduct in early 1960 had contributed to his fall and months of political uncertainty. But a decade had passed by the time Park confronted Washington with another military seizure; in 1972 unlike 1961, the threat of Chinese intervention was completely discounted, and, in fact, Washington had already begun the process of normalization of relations with Peking. Moreover, the north no longer was the threat she had been ten years earlier, and in any case could not count on unqualified support from her patrons. What the United States also knew, but chose to disregard, was that, unlike other countries where it was confronted by the government on one side and radical leftist challengers on the other, the opposition in Seoul was more attached to democratic institutions, and thus closer related to American national interests than was the party in power. No case could conceivably be made that in Korea the opposition Democratic party was leftist or anti-American. For with Koreans of whatever political persuasion, communism was not an attractive ideological option. Preoccupation with Vietnam clouded top-level Washington thinking, especially that emanating from the White House. Park was contributing to the effort of the United States in Vietnam. Surely he deserved more than the back of the hand from Washington?

The Inevitable Comparison to the North

Finally, we should consider the status of human rights in North Korea. While little was known about life in the north, reports which came out with the few Western journalists and travelers who had been permitted to visit provided the image of a rigorous thought-controlled revolutionary government that made eastern Europe's brand of communism liberal by comparison. In the north there was not even the semblance of representative institutions, opposition political parties, free elections, free press, or any of those human righs which dissidents in the south were able at least to demand. There was no argument between the Department of State and human rights activists on this score; both recognized the deplorable status of freedoms in the North.[18] If they disagreed, it was only with respect to the relevance of this fact for U.S. support of the Park regime. Washington has not spilled blood on behalf of Pyongyang's causes, nor defended it with military force, nor lavished it with enormous assistance. Notwithstanding, the rejoinder "But what about human rights in the north?" is always raised whenever the argument is made for a more forceful American role in the south.

NATIONAL SECURITY: REAL OR FANCIED

Security, as more than one American secretary of state seemed to conclude, has lately become an important, in fact overriding, element in determining the response of the United States to South Korea's repressive conduct.[19] To what extent was human rights considered in the formulation of foreign policy towards Korea? To answer that question I turn to three critical events involving human rights.

The 1960-1962 Political Upheaval

Between 1960 and 1962 Korea moved from the authoritarianism of Syngman Rhee to the unrestrained freedom of Chang Myun's government and then back to repression under Major-General Park Chung-hee. In 1960 the Korean War had been over only a few short years; mainland China was viewed as a provocative belligerent; and in Europe the United States seemed on a collision course with the Soviet Union. Yet even in these circumstances of unquestioned risk to national security, Secretary Herter called in the South Korean ambassador and in as plain and direct an American reaction to the denial of human righs in an allied country as is on record bluntly informed him that the repressive actions taken by Syngman Rhee "were unsuited to a free democracy."[20] Herter than made his views known publicly. He was not intimidated by any concern for security, nor were his representations shrouded in secrecy; the time for so-called "quiet diplomacy" had passed. What the United States had to say about repression in Korea it said directly, forcefully, and openly, and Rhee fell in part because of this stand.

Then in August 1960 the Chang Myun government was elected. It took office as the result of the first truly free expression of the popular will since Korea had become a republic. The United States was hailed as having clearly demonstrated its belief in human rights, in this instance at a time when other considerations might well have subordinated moral values. Yet just a year later, the United States faced a similarly perplexing challenge; this time it failed to uphold respect for human rights and in so doing lost all it had gained by its earlier forthright position. That is, in May 1961 Park Chung-hee, a little-known Korean military officer with questionable credentials struck against Chang's government. (Park had been cashiered from the South Korean Army for participation in the communist-inspired 1948 Yosu rebellion; he was subsequently reinstated at the time of the Korean War.) Marshall Green, then chargé d'affaires, had had little difficulty in determining where the national interests of the United States lay. Within six hours after the coup began, on his own initiative, he issued a statement making "emphatically clear" that the United States remained squarely behind the elected government which had come to power through free and fair elections. This time Washington lacked the courage of its convictions.

President John Kennedy had been in office only four months. Saddled with responsibility for the Bay of Pigs fiasco, overly cautious lest he find himself involved in another disaster in foreign affairs and unfortunately on a state visit to Canada at the time of the coup, Kennedy reacted indecisively to the statement of his chargé in Seoul. The absence from Washington of the Secretary of State as well as the Undersecretary further discouraged a strong response against the violation. Whatever, Washington's unwillingness promptly to support the Embassy pulled the rug out from under Green's principled stance. Was the issue of popular will as manifested by a democratic election weighed against national security? In Seoul the Embassy conclusion was that the United States had little choice but to stand against illegal seizure of a government it put forward in Asia as a "showcase of democracy." In Washington those in leadership were not prepared or willing to bolster a democratically elected government. There is no evidence that the question was human rights versus national security; rather it was a case of diplomatic ineptitude euphemistically called "wait and see."

1972 Constitutional Amendment

In mid-October 1972 President Park justified martial law in terms of the changed international situation (the Nixon visit to China in February of 1972, the China-Japan rapprochement of September, the defeat of the United States in Vietnam) as well as the alleged need for an all-out disciplined effort to confront the North Korean threat. (Three months earlier Park had led his country into an agreement with North Korea for bilateral talks on a peaceful approach to unification; North Korea in the fall of 1972 thus was hardly cause for martial law.) Essentially what was at stake was Park's authority and power in what he had promised would be his last term of office.

The American Embassy in Seoul was given only a few hours advance notice of Park's coup. It recommended that unless Washington was prepared to cut off economic and military aid, it had no recourse but to acquiesce in Park's action while not publicly becoming a part of it. (It was at this time that the overworked reaction to repression in Korea—"we are neither involved nor associated"—came into being.) To the White House and the National Security Council, the unkindest blow was Park's rationalization that the Nixon-Kissinger initiatives towards China and Vietnam were undermining

Asian security. Nixon was still walking a tight wire with the Republican party on the China opening and his efforts to get out of Vietnam "with honor" were precariously balanced; Park's gratuitous allusions were hardly helpful. So it was basically to those references that the response of the United States was directed. Acting under instructions, Ambassador Phillip Habib was somewhat successful in persuading Park to water down his intended public explanation, particularly regarding Vietnam. The White House was not interested in confronting Park over the mass destruction of constitutional guarantees for human rights.

Then, in January 1973 Prime Minister Kim Chong-pil met President Nixon on the occasion of ex-president Truman's death. Park had dispatched Kim to Washington as much to test Washington's reaction as to express condolences on the passing of an American president whose decision in June 1950 saved the South Korean people. Kim's real objective was to convince Nixon that Park's actions were expedients required to meet challenges from the north. Nixon responded that he had no intention of interfering in the internal affairs of Korea.[21] Given the circumstances it had the effect of encouraging Park to proceed further with one-man government.

Once more the problem of human rights, this time represented in its broadest constitutional dimension, was not addressed by the State Department or the White House. Certainly no one in either place believed that Park's actions were due to the North Korean threat. To the contrary, the American Embassy and Washington both recognized that basically what was involved was a simple grab for greater power. But it came at a time when Nixon and Kissinger, neither of whom betrayed a strong commitment to human rights issues, had other priorities in mind, priorities which had little to do with the North Korean "threat." And they were not about to engage in a public quarrel with Park which they believed could have had serious implications for the credibility of their diplomatic initiatives in Vietnam.

1974 Emergency Measures

By the end of 1973 Park faced a rising demand for restoration of constitutional liberties in Korea from opposition politicians, intellectuals, students, and particularly by Christian church leaders. He responded by turning legal jurisdiction over to military courts, and once more raised the spectre of "the threat."

In the Department of State, the Office of Korean Affairs was attempting to formulate the response to Park's latest repression against a rigid White House and Kissingerian intolerance of human-rights advocates. In January 1974, at a top-level review of overall policy towards Korea, Kissinger (now Secretary of State) made clear that what took place internally in Korea was no business of the United States. This view also was repeated on several occasions by Kissinger, who prevailed over the Office of Korean Affairs, which had deplored Park's actions, and Ambassador Habib. When certain of Habib's actions became known to Kissinger however, he was bluntly instructed in the spring of 1974 to "get off the backs" of Park's government. So dominant were Kissinger's views on human rights that notwithstanding the repressive events in Korea (which had resulted in a special hearing by the Fraser Subcommittee in the House of Representatives) President Ford could not find reason to avoid a trip to Korea when on his visit to Vladyvostok in the fall of 1974. In fact, had he searched in his briefing book he would have been hard put to find any mention at all about the status of human rights in Korea.

POLICY OPTIONS AND LEVERAGE

Since 1950, critics of repressive regimes in Korea have called for removal of American forces, or reduction in military or bilateral economic assistance; occasionally there have been calls for trade or other economic sanctions. In response, policy-makers have argued that the north is a threat to South Korea, and therefore that the government of South Korea must be supported to forestall that threat, no matter how repressive it might be. What are the risks or chance of success in these options? Are there others that could be tried? Or should the United States stop worrying altogether about Korea and hope that its impressive economic development will eventually resolve the problem?

The U.S. Military Presence

American military forces were stationed on the Korea peninsula because of security considerations and their future presence should depend primarily on such factors. When the Korean War ended, American troops remained to serve as a shield behind which the Republic of Korea could develop economically and politically. This military presence has served the economic objective well; for over a quarter century it made possible an opportunity for the Korean economy to boom.

There is little evidence that the American military presence has contributed to the political development in the south. Admittedly, it can be argued that by preventing war and the possible domination by the north, the United States may have helped preserve the form if not the substance of democratic institutions in the south.

Yet American troops have fulfilled an important political mission, serving as a reminder to the north of the intention and capacity of the United States to respond in case of conflict. For this purpose, however, 32,000 ground troops are no longer required. In fact, as was argued by the State Department when the South Korean government contested the withdrawal of 20,000 troops in 1971, all that is required to invoke the commitment of the United States is one American soldier, a grim reminder that one American casualty along the DMZ could plunge the United States into hostilities with the north.

Some observers have speculated that the military presence of the United States may have served another political purpose, namely restraining Park from becoming even more repressive.[22] This, however, may be readily dismissed. There is no evidence that Park was ever restrained in his march toward authoritarianism by concern that the United States might react with force reductions. To the contrary, a more telling argument is that Park has used the military presence of the United States as a visible reminder to his opposition that regardless of their dissidence, the United States supports him.

Even accepting the recently revised reassessment of the North Korean military line-up (an assumption not without question), for reasons previously examined, North Korea is hardly the threat it formerly was. What remains of the threat can be contained by the south, with, for the time being, the aid of American air power. Accordingly, the question of whether or not to keep American ground troops on the peninsula can be separated from the human-rights issue and resolved on its merits. Moreover, to link a military presence of the United States with the status of human rights can lead to illogical determinations. If, for example, American forces were removed solely because of South Korea's repressive conduct, should they be returned under a truly democratic regime?

In any case, the Carter Administration has decided to bypass the issue of linkage. The United States will withdraw ground troops over a four to five-year period by 1982 leaving behind the air wing. Before that, however, there will be a gradual scaling down in the size and composition of ground forces, possibly to brigade size (as was originally planned by the Joint Chiefs of Staff in 1971). Given the rate of the south's military buildup, the continuance of the air wing beyond this period will also become difficult to justify. Certainly will this be true should the Carter Administration go through with its commitment in "principle" to provide Korea with 60 F-16's, a high performance aircraft that in technology at least goes beyond anything in either the inventory of the South or the North. (Such a determination is fraught with the gravest of consequences for an arms race on the Korean peninsula that could make the issue of human rights pale in comparison. At least one indication of a Soviet desire to avoid such escalation may be noted in its restraint in not placing its own sophisticated MIG 23 in the North's arsenal—assistance it has not hesitated to provide other friends.)

Military Assistance

The case regarding military assistance to Korea is much the same as that regarding the stationing of forces with, however, one important difference. Section 502B of the International Security Assistance Act of 1976 provides that "except under circumstances specified in this section, no security assistance may be provided to any country the government of which engages in a consistent pattern of gross violations of internationally recognized human rights." Opportunity exists for the Department of State to justify those "extraordinary circumstances" which necessitate a continuation of security assistance.

Human rights has thus been linked in law to security assistance. Unless the State Department can make a case to the contrary, military assistance to Korea should be eliminated or, as a minimum, restricted in amount. The only "extraordinary circumstances" which could apply relate to the so-called threat. But as indicated, considering all elements, the economic and international as well as military, the south is today more than a match for its northern rival. Moreover, by the end of FY 1980 if not before, the alleged gap in the air will have been remedied thus ending any plausible claim that imbalances justifying "extraordinary circumstances" exist.

Two additional arguments have frequently been made against the use of military assistance as leverage. First, Park would go elsewhere for his military hardware; and second, that South Korea is now using her own money and no longer procuring through grant aid from the United States. Therefore, why not go along with Park? Both arguments are specious; they are put forward by Seoul's advocates to undermine the case against Korea.

To begin with, since 1950 the United States has spent almost $7 billion equipping the Korean armed forces; the stamp "U.S. made" is conspicuous throughout the South's military arsenal. For Korea to turn to other arms producers at this date, probably Western Europe, would seriously complicate the system of operation and maintenance (spare parts) and obstruct the modernization process. The United States is easily the most efficient and reliable arms manufacturer in the West and its technological lead is overwhelming, especially in the air. And while it is true that Seoul is accelerating an indigenous arms industry, it will be some time, if ever, before South Korea will be independent of the military "know-how" of the United States. In the meanwhile, Seoul does not intend to remain second class in matters of defense. Yet whenever the United States has delayed Park's military orders, there emanates from Seoul a barrage of carefully leaked intelligence that he is shopping elsewhere. This ploy, orchestrated in tune with the sales efforts of American munitions makers, has had effective results with the Pentagon and the Congress.

Second, while it is true that annual grant military assistance did end for all practical purposes in 1976 (except, of course, for the exceptional grant of $800 million as "compensation" under Carter's troop withdrawal plan), credit financing and commercial sales, which have taken its place, are not without substantial cost to the United States treasury. Guaranteed credit terms require congressional appropriation (one-tenth of the total credits), and such credit is more generous than commercial terms. Moreover, there are many intangible costs to the taxpayer in maintaining the Pentagon and State Department overhead structure that focuses a sizeable portion of its worldwide assistance effort on Korea, including the licensing for export of military goods bought commercially. To say that credit or even cash purchase is at no charge to the United States government is to gloss over sizeable hidden costs.

What would be the effect of a determination by the United States to cut off or to seriously limit military

assistance in accordance with Section 502B? In all likelihood, the political ramifications would be more sensitive
than the military. The North Korean threat is the most
cited reason why such action should not be taken. But
North Korea has enough major internal problems to
refrain from aggressive action until certain at least of
support from her allies, and until the longer range implications of the decision made by the United States
became clearer. The Chinese and the Soviets would
most likely counsel patience and recommend diplomatic
initiatives with the United States (in fact there is reason
to believe this is what the Chinese have been doing);
there would be no greater incentive to them to support
military action then than now. In fact, given the Soviet
desires for a SALT treaty, and China's preoccupation
with modernization, less. Japan would pause to reflect
but would watch and wait for further developments.
The internal political restraints that presently serve to
keep Japan from increasing the size of her military or
going nuclear would continue to operate. Japan's contribution to defense, which is now less than 1 percent of its
G.N.P. might be increased, but this is likely to occur in
any event. Obviously, Japan should be consulted; but
in all likelihood, she would not be pressed to quick
reaction.

The most immediate impact would be on South
Korea's internal political line-up. If the decision to eliminate or cut military assistance deeply (including cash
sales) were conveyed as representing the united view of
the United States government, shared in by the president and a majority in Congress, President Park would
be in trouble. A firm display of displeasure by the
United States with Park's conduct would seriously complicate his maneuverability with the military and large
domestic business interests whose personal fortunes are

dependent on ties with the United States. He would have but one choice as concerns human rights: moderate while trying to hold on to the presidency. In all likelihood, his days would be numbered no matter how he reacted. If he were removed from office, he would probably be replaced in short order by a military-civilian coalition. If he did not relax his rule but rather attempted to buy his military goods elsewhere, it is likely that he still would be replaced. Domestically, Park's potential weakness is the attitude of his military. If his armed forces became convinced that his adamancy on human rights was moving Korea away from the military commitment and political support of the United States, Park could be expendable.

Following this speculative scenario further, is the removal of Park an unacceptable risk? Admittedly, not all change can be accomplished without disturbance. Syngman Rhee's passing was accompanied by limited internal turbulence. However, scenarios detailing succession are as unpredictable as they are popular; in few instances have changes in office gone according to rational predictions. But in judging South Korea the possibilities are not all that great. Park cannot, as can some of his Asian neighbors, play the Chinese off against the Soviets, nor can he look to Japan for defense. He also cannot hope to go it alone and keep up the momentum of growth. Korea's benefactor is the United States: in military commitment and support, in political endorsement at the U.N. and in world capitals, and in trade and development assistance. For this reason, the Korean government, while pretending to be otherwise, is deeply troubled by Carter's expressions on human rights and his professed intention to curb arms sales worldwide. In this circumstance it is inconceivable that anyone replacing Park Chung-hee could come from more reactionary circles or would move to greater repression. The far greater likelihood is that the military and political leadership would form an interim coalition while restoring important aspects of the previous constitution (particularly rights and freedoms), providing for a return to direct election of a president and moving to restore the confidence of the United States. Easily, the one element that would give no concern to any new administration would be the economy, short, of course, of armed conflict on the peninsula. South Korea has the experienced managerial skill, and the reservoir of scientific and technical talent needed for continued industrial development.

Economic Assistance

Bilateral direct governmental economic assistance to Korea is mainly carried out under Title 1, PL 480 whereby agricultural commodities are sold at concessionary terms involving long-term repayment and low rates of interest. Such aid to Korea would have been phased out by now were it not for the highly questionable secret commitment entered into by former President Nixon to induce the South Korean government voluntarily to reduce textile exports to the United States.[23]

Notwithstanding its intention to use food-for-peace, the PL 480 program is frequently utilized as a convenient solution to domestic farm pressures, particularly agricultural surplus. Because of the farm vote, and the emotional appeal of "food for the needy," Congress is reluctant to use any leverage it possesses under PL 480. In addition, efforts to cut PL 480 for Korea because of human rights failed badly in Congress in mid-1976, and there is little chance they would fare better in the future.

Moreover, even if Congress were to find the votes to apply such restrictions, Korea would hardly be hurt. It could, without too much difficulty turn to commercial channels for grain purchases, and so far as rice is concerned, probably to other countries.

But Korea is dependent on the United States for substantial economic assistance through a variety of credits, guarantees, and insurance, the denial or obstruction of which would have a great impact on that country and cause her leaders to reflect seriously about human rights. Some 11 agencies supported by the United States government furnished $1.37 billion in economic assistance in FY 1976.[24]

Obviously, the United States has an enormous influence on Korea's economic growth. If the United States decided to apply this influence to assure human rights, it would avoid the largely emotional argument surrounding military assistance and national security.

Would use of this leverage be apt to force a change? In large part this would depend on the way the message was sent. If the United States informed South Korea diplomatically but firmly that it would look more sympathetically on requests for economic assistance from countries adhering to acceptable human rights standards, South Korea would agree to guarantee them. But, if it did not, the United States could reject an Export-Import credit application, or vote against (rather than abstaining, which has been the more usual practice) a multilateral loan, which would soon make the seriousness of the policy clear.

To a United States, long inclined to indulge the aberrations of conduct by so-called friendly governments, such action may appear overly strong. But, in 1975, when South Korea was determined to purchase a French nuclear reprocessing plant capable of converting fuel to weapons-grade plutonium, the United States was not hesitant to use such economic pressure. Worried that South Korea was moving toward a nuclear option, the United States made Korea realize that future financing decisions were contingent on Seoul's decision, including future credits like those from the Export-Import Bank for a second $292 million Westinghouse atomic power reactor plant already under construction.[25] The United States also persuaded Canada to hold up the sale of another nuclear plant. As a result, Seoul cancelled the purchase. Whether a nuclear weapon orientation is more serious than gross violations of human rights is not the issue. The question is does the United States have the economic influence to achieve a given objective? So far as Korea is concerned the answer has been demonstrated. What has not been demonstrated, however, is that the Carter administration is prepared to use its economic muscle in behalf of human rights in Korea.

Conventional Diplomacy

Under Kissinger the Department of State professed an attachment to moral values and claimed to pursue its human rights objective through "quiet diplomacy and counsel." Its accomplishments in South Korea were negligible. It failed not because such diplomacy is typically ineffective but rather because both the private and the public record of the White House and Secretary of State on human rights negated any possibility of gains through such means. It does not take a foreign government long to determine that a representation by a lesser-ranking diplomatic officer simply reflects form and hardly the serious concern of the White House, and especially so when put in context of inconsistent action by the executive branch.

When, a few weeks after Park jettisoned the constitution, President Nixon in a meeting with the South Korean Prime Minister deliberately ignored the act, the Korean government could only conclude that representations made earlier were largely pro forma. And when, following the mass arrests and trials of 1974, President Ford continued to call for increased military assistance and chose to visit Seoul, these earlier reactions were confirmed.

The known disinterest of Kissinger for human-rights issues completely undermined any possible effectiveness those concerned in the department might have had. In fact, subjecting their views and representations to ridicule (as in Kissinger's responses to his envoys in Korea and Chile) created a climate of intimidation wherein few were prepared to speak out or take initiatives to accredit a role in foreign policy for human rights. Yet, given the full support of the White House, conventional diplomacy can be helpful. Speeches and press interviews by the president underscoring human rights, letters to foreign governments and meetings called by the White House with foreign dignitaries to emphasize a presidential concern, go a considerable way towards demonstrating at the highest level a sense of moral principles in the United States. Admittedly, however, the effectiveness of diplomatic representations is limited to protesting the instances of arbitrary arrest and conviction rather than the systemic roots of repression. To address the large problem of coup, martial law, and constitutional abandonment, a quiet rejoinder or expression is inadequate. In such cases, congressional action to reduce or eliminate economic and military assistance, or rejection of a loan application by the president registers more effectively the American sense of outrage over undemocratic behavior which cannot be ignored, misunderstood or misinterpreted.

Initiatives Towards North Korea

Another diplomatic initiative the United States should consider concerns relations with the north. For too long, the United States has allowed her reactions to Kim Il-Sung's overtures to be hostage to the south. For example the United States will not enter into discussions with the north save in the presence of the south. While this condition may have served a purpose initially in helping the south gain self-confidence, it no longer seems valid or required, nor given the conduct of the south, desireable. In effect, it allows the south a veto over American initiatives or responses that might reduce tensions with the north and also nudge the south toward a more relaxed position on human rights. South Korea should be made to know that in the eyes of many Americans, its conduct does not entitle it to any special favor or privileges. In fact for many Americans the distinctions between the undemocratic conduct of a dictatorial Kim Il-Sung and that of an authoritarian Park Chung-hee are becoming increasing blurred.

VIII. Conclusions

1) *Security has been an overworked rationalization for avoiding human rights initiatives in South Korea.* This is not to deny that over the past two decades North Korea has been provocative, or that Kim Il-Sung's central hope remains unification of the peninsula under his banner.

Rather, it is to say that while the United States has recognized that North Korea is unable to dominate the peninsula, it has not been willing to factor this conclusion into diplomacy with the South. The U.S. has frequently spoken with pride of the "economic miracle" of the South, and with derision of the economic problems of the North, but it has not publicly offset the North's capacity for trouble in terms of the great economic disparity between the two. Similarly has this been true of the respective military capacities of north and south.

Over the years the U.S. has sought to justify its military presence on the Korean peninsula by whatever means appeared rational, each time postponing the inevitable reductions and withdrawal of forces. While the draw-down of 20,000 troops in FY 1971 was met with temper tantrums from Park, it was not accompanied by aggressive reactions from the North. The case advanced by some—that this force reduction led to Park's determination to centralize power—does not hold. In fact, it merely gave him another excuse to justify an action that was inevitable from the time he first seized the government in 1961. This also may be noted in the way he sought to use for personal ambition the opening of U.S. discussions with China—certainly the most hopeful step towards peace in Asia in a quarter of a century.

When it became obvious in 1972-1973 that the U.S. would soon be faced with a military withdrawal from Vietnam, the Pentagon looked for other reasons to justify a military presence in Asia. Korea offered the best facilities: a government that desired a U.S. presence and bases already in place. For a short period a case was advanced for a "mobile Division" positioned in South Korea and ready to defend U.S. interests anywhere in the Pacific area. But this trial balloon was shot down quickly. The U.S. military presence on the Korean peninsula was soon back to being jusitfied on the basis of the North Korea threat, embellished, of course, by a still continuing political rationale.

What this review of developments on the Korean peninsula over the past decade and a half seems to indicate is that national security, while certainly a concern, was not the dominant reason for downgrading initiatives in human rights. It was not the reason in 1961 when the U.S. hesitated, nor was it in 1972 and 1974. While the actual reasons, as noted earlier, varied from the 1960's to the 1970's, what does seem clear is that in none of these instances did Washington evaluate the human rights problem versus the security consideration and then conclude that the latter was of overriding consequence.

2) In the Korean context, linkage of the *military presence* to human rights unnecessarily complicates the argument over how to take the latter into account. *The presence of U.S. forces on the Korean peninsula should be geared solely to the security needs. And in those terms reduction of U.S. ground troops is overdue.* The process of reduction began in 1971 can be completed without jeopardy within the next three years, as President Carter has pledged. Withdrawal should be accompanied by discussions with the Soviets and the Chinese as well as the Japanese in the search for some solution to the Korean question other than a perpetual arms race. The opportunity for such discussion did not exist in 1971. Today it does, and it should be fully exploited.

3) *In terms of Section 502B of the current security assistance legislation, the U.S. Congress has no alternative but to restrict military assistance to South Korea because of its record of gross violation of human rights.* The case made to date by the Administration is not convincing evidence of "extraordinary circumstances." The Department of State has not

only continued to overemphasize or allow to be exaggerated the security threat, but worse still it has continued to minimize the deprivation of human rights in the South. Congress in Section 502B has legislated a requirement for a "full and complete report" regarding the status of human rights in each country proposed as a recipient of security assistance. The facts presented by the State Department in response to this requirement are not only inadequate and inconsistent with earlier reporting, but read like an attorney's brief for the defendant. Indeed, any summary of the status of human rights in Korea which does not include reference to the kidnapping of Kim Tae-chung fails by any standard of objectivity to be full and complete.

4) Probably the most effective source of influence over Korea could be her continuing need for U.S. economic assistance. Moreover, the application of this influence would avoid the quagmire of the security argument and thus focus directly on Korea's requirements for development assistance funds, trade credits, and investment guarantees. The case may be made that Korea will turn to private American and international banking institutions. So be it. But at least the U.S. government will be spared the pain and embarrassment of underwriting repression in Korea. *The U.S. should apply this leverage forcefully after close review of projects proposed, selecting first those which have lesser impact on the poor and needy.* Consideration might first be given to Export-Import credits, OPIC guarantees, and World Bank Loans.

5) To emphasize that the U.S. does in fact hold Park's repressive acts to be repugnant to the American sense of moral values, as President Carter stated before entering the White House, *the U.S. government must take steps that have public visibility.* Forthright State Department comment on the status of human rights in Korea would be

the minimum required, and far more desirable would be statements directly attributable to the President. No better beginning for a more responsible and responsive policy could be found than with regard to Kim Tae-chung. The U.S. has been a silent witness for too long to Kim's kidnapping by the Korean CIA. In a moral, if not legal, sense, the U.S. has a responsibility to this persecuted man. A letter to Kim from the President expressing interest in his welfare and inviting him to the U.S. would be a good way to demonstrate our concern.

What is required is not quiet counsel which has served to obscure silent, and too frequently, deceptive diplomacy. What is sorely needed in our relations with Korea is visible diplomacy which Park Chung-hee and the Korean and American public can see and understand.

NOTES

1. *A Historical Summary of United States-Korean Relations,* (Washington: Department of State, November, 1962) pp. 52-53.
2. See prepared statement of William J. Butler, entitled "Report of Commission to South Korea for Amnesty International," in *Human Rights in South Korea, Hearings Before the Subcommittee on Asian and Pacific Affairs and on International Organizations and Movements of the Committee on Foreign Affairs,* House of Representatives, 93rd Congress, July 30, August 5, and December 20, 1974, p. 41.
3. For an authoritative account of Kim's kidnapping see Don Oberdorfer, "The Case of the Kidnapped Korea," *The Washington Post* (August 26, 1973), p. C-3; and Donald L. Ranard, "Japan's Responsibility in Kim Dae-Jung Affair," *Mainichi Daily News* (Tokyo, August 10, 1978); see also account by Kim Hyung-wook, former Director, KCIA in "Investigation of Korean-American Relations," *Hearings*

Before the Subcommittee on International Organizations of the Committee on International Relations, Part 1, June 22, 1977, 95th Congress, 1st Session.

4. There is considerable question as to the reliability of data regarding arrests and convictions under the emergency measures. For example, in July 1974 the State Department testified that 55 persons had been convicted under measure No. 4 (nine to death, 19 to life, and the balance to prison for periods from 15 to 20 years), and that 36 had been sentenced under Emergency Measure No. 1. Yet, in its report to Congress required under Section 502b of the 1976 Foreign Assistance Act, the State Department indicated in March 1977 that under all 1974 measures 35 persons were found guilty.

5. See *Hearings,* 93rd Congress, op.cit., especially testimony by Arthur Hummel, Acting Assistant Secretary of State for East Asian and Pacific Affairs; also see testimony by William Butler, same hearings. Further accusations concerning torture are contained in the testimony of Jerome Alan Cohen, Director of East Asian Legal Studies, Harvard Law School; Brian Wrobel, Amnesty International, and Donald L. Ranard, former Director, Office of Korean Affairs, Department of State, in *Hearings Before the Subcommittee on International Organizations of the Committee on International Relations,* House of Representatives, 94th Congress, May 20-22, June 3, 5, 10, 12, 17 and 24, 1975.

6. See "Report on An Amnesty International Mission to the Republic of Korea, March 27-April 9, 1975," in *Hearings,* 1975, op.cit.

7. John K.C. Oh, "South Korea 1975: A Permanent Emergency," *Asian Survey* (January, 1976); also "Report on an Amnesty International Mission to the Republic of Korea," op. cit.

8. Peter Weintraub, "Critical Days in Kim's Pyongyang," *Far Eastern Economic Review* (November 5, 1976), pp. 11-14.

9. For years, military analysts placed North Korean ground forces at roughly 440,000. In January 1979 the *Army Times* reported a dramatic increase in the North Korean order

of battle. There is, however, some reason to question the upsurge (that is, the difficulty of estimating armed forces in a country as closed as North Korea). See *Korea: The U.S. Troop Withdrawal,* Report of the Pacific Study Group to the Committee on Armed Services, United States Senate, January 23, 1979. For an earlier study, see Stefan Leader, "An Assessment of the Korean Military Situation," *Defense Monograph* (Washington, D.C.: Center for Defense Information, April 1976).

10. For a review of Kim Il-Sung's economic problems, see Lee Chong-sik, "New Paths for North Korea," *Problems of Communism* (March-April, 1977); as well as "Letter from Pyongyang," *Far Eastern Economic Review* (September 15, 1978). Also see Weintraub, op.cit., and Bernard Nossiter, "The Gang That Couldn't Smuggle Right," *The Washington Post* (October 31, 1976).

11. For a comprehensive analysis of United States military assistance to Korea, as well as Korean defense spending see the Korea section of *Human Rights and the U.S. Foreign Assistance Program, Fiscal Year 1978, Part II* (Washington, D.C.: Center for International Policy, October 1977).

12. The United States Arms Control and Disarmament Agency, *World Military Expenditures and Arms Trade, 1966-1975* (Washington, D.C.); also *Korea: The Economic Race Between the North and the South* (Washington, D.C.: National Foreign Assessment Center, Central Intelligence Agency, January 1978); and "South Korea '79," *Far Eastern Economic Review* (May 18, 1979). See "Aid to South Korea Said Twice That Given To North," *The Washington Post* (August 9, 1977); also "South Korean Economic Outlook Bullish Despite Carter's Plans To Pull Out Troops," *The Wall Street Journal* (August 30, 1977). Donald S. Zagoria and Young Kun Kim in their essay, "North Korea and the Major Powers," included in *Two Koreas in East Asian Affairs* (New York: New York University Press, 1976) have compiled statistics on North Korea's economic problems which argue to them that the remarkable progress in the South "is bound to have a sobering effect on Pyongyang."

13. *Korea Week,* Vol. 10, no. 4 (March 9, 1977), has a good review on various press and scholarly reporting on the so-called power struggle in North Korea.

14. Lee Chong-sik, op. cit.

15. Edwin O. Reischauer, "Time for a New American Policy on Korea," *The Christian Science Monitor* (July 26, 1976).

16. Don Oberdorfer, "Carter, Japan's Fukuda End Talks Without Agreement on Nuclear Fuel," *The Washington Post* (March 23, 1977).

17. Letter from Edwin O. Reischauer to Congressman Don Fraser (D-Minnesota) December 12, 1975, commenting favorably on a proposed Fraser-Solarz amendment to withdraw American troops from Korea.

18. For recent testimony on this, see "Human Rights in North Korea,"*Hearings Before the Subcommittee on International Organizations of the Committee on International Relations,* House of Representatives, 94th Congress, September 9, 1976.

19. See Don Oberdorfer, "Vance, in Human Rights Push, Asks Cuts in Aid to 3 Nations," *The Washington Post* (February 25, 1977).

20. "A Historical Summary of United States-Korean Relationships," op. cit., p. 131.

21. For an account of Nixon-Kissinger reactions to internal developments in Korea see Don Oberdorfer, "U.S. Reportedly Tolerated S. Korean Rights Abuses," *The Washington Post* (May 17, 1976). Oberdorfer's article resulted from an extensive interview with the author, and is a substantially accurate representation of the author's views.

22. Ralph N. Clough, *Deterence and Defense in Korea* (Washington, D.C.: The Brookings Institution, 1976), p. 31.

23. As part of the Republican party "southern strategy" to break into the solid South during the 1968 presidential election, Nixon committed himself to reducing the import of textiles which was causing unemployment and distress to the Southern textile industry. Subsequently in 1970 and 1971 Nixon sent former Treasury Secretary David

Kennedy to Taiwan, Japan, and Korea to negotiate a voluntary agreement to cut back their textile exports to the United States. The agreement with Korea which was negotiated privately by Kennedy without State Department and AID input and not submitted to Congress, cost the United States $485 million in PL 480 payments over a five-year period and $100 million in reduced local currency-use payments. See *Report of the Comptroller General of the United States,* "U.S. Agreements With The Republic of Korea," February 20, 1976.

24. For an illuminating study of American aid, including that contributed to South Korea see James R. Morrell, "Foreign Aid: Evading the Control of Congress," *International Policy Report,* Vol. III, No. 1 (Washington, D.C.: Center for International Policy, January 1977).

25. Don Oberdorfer, "South Korea Cancels A-Plant," *The Washington Post* (January 30, 1976).

BIBLIOGRAPHY

Arnson, Cynthia, and William Goodfellow. "OPEC: Insuring the Status Quo." *International Policy Report,* Vol. III No. 2. Washington, D.C.: Center for International Policy, September 1977.

Association of the U.S. Army. "Korea in Context—A Primer on the Dynamics of Northeast Asia," inserted in the *Congressional Record,* July 25, 1977, p. S 12743.

Barnds, William J., ed. *The Two Koreas In East Asian Affairs.* New York: New York University Press, 1976.

———. "The U.S. and South Korea: Surmounting the Crisis." *Worldview,* July/August 1977.

Center for International Policy. *Human Rights and the U.S. Foreign Assistance Program,* Fiscal Year 1978, Part II—East Asia. Washington, D.C., October 1977.

Clough, Ralph N. *Deterrence and Defense in Korea.* Washington, D.C.: The Brookings Institution, 1976.

Emergency Christian Conference on Korean Problems. *Documents on the Struggle for Democracy in Korea.* Tokyo: Shinkyo Shuppansha, 1975.

"South Korea 79." *Far Eastern Economic Review* (May 18, 1979).

Fraser, Donald M. "Freedom and Foreign Policy." *Foreign Policy,* No. 26, Spring, 1977.

Gibney, Frank. "The Ripple Effect in Korea." *Foreign Affairs,* October 1977.

Hasan, Parvez. "Korea, Problems and Issues in a Rapidly Growing Economy." Baltimore: The Johns Hopkins University Press, 1976.

Kim, Jin-hyun. "Pedalling Faster in Hot Pursuit of Growth Targets." *The Far Eastern Economic Review,* May 20, 1977.

Leader, Stafan. "An Assessment of the Korean Military Situation." *Defense Monograph,* Washington, D.C.: Center for Defense Information, April 1976.

Lee Chong-sik. "New Paths for North Korea." Problems of Communism, March-April 1977.

McGovern, Senator George M. "A Durable Peace in Korea— The Challenge to U.S. Policy," address to conference of Japanese and American parliamentarians. Washington, D.C. September 19, 1976.

————. "The U.S. Risk in Korea." *Defense Review,* No. 2, 1977.

Morrell, James. "Foreign Aid: Evading the Control of Congress." *International Policy Report,* Vol. III, No. 1, January 1977.

Nelson, Lars-Erick. "Park Has Dismantled Democracy" (an interview with Congressman Donald M. Fraser). *Newsweek,* July 11, 1977.

Ranard, Donald L. "What We Should Do About Korea." *Worldview,* June 1976.

————. "The U.S. in Korea: What Price Security?" *Worldview,* January/February 1977.

Rowan, Roy. "There's Also Some Good News About South Korea." *Fortune,* September 1977.

Spurr, Russell. "A Chill Wind from Carter's Washington." Also "The Jitters on Freedom's Frontier." *Far Eastern Economic Review,* May 6, 1977.

Szulc, Tad. "Inside South Korea's CIA." *New York Times Magazine,* March 6, 1977.

U.S. Arms Control and Disarmament Agency. *World Military Expenditures and Arms Transfers 1966-1975.* Washington, D.C.

U.S. Congress. House. Committee on Foreign Affairs. Subcommittees on Asian and Pacific Affairs and on International Organizations and Movements. *Human Rights in South Korea: Implications for U.S. Policy.* Hearings, July, August and December, 1974. 93rd Congress, 2nd Session.

U.S. Congress. House. Committee on International Relations. Subcommittee on International Organizations. *Human Rights in South Korea and the Philippines: Implications for U.S. Policy.* Hearings, May and June 1975. 94th Congress, 1st Session.

————. *Activities of the Korean Central Intelligence Agency in the United States.* Hearings, March 1976. 94th Congress, 2nd Session.

————. *Human Rights in North Korea.* Hearings, September 9, 1976. 94th Congress, 2nd Session.

————. *Investigation of Korean-American Relations.* Hearings, June 22, 1977. 95th Congress, 1st Session.

U.S. Congress. House. Committee on International Relations. Subcommittee on Asian and Pacific Affairs. *Report of a Special Study Mission to Asia, April 8-21, 1977.* June 19, 1977. 95th Congress, 1st Session.

U.S. Congress. Senate. Committee on Foreign Relations. Subcommittee on Foreign Assistance. *Human Rights Reports.* Prepared by the Department of State in accordance with Section 502(B) of the Foreign Assistance Act, as amended, March 1977. 95th Congress, 1st Session.

U.S. General Accounting Office. *U.S. Agreements With The Republic of Korea.* Report of the Comptroller General of the United States. February 20, 1970.

Vance, Cyrus, Secretary of State. "United States and Asia." (Speech before the Asia Society.) New York, June 29, 1977.

Weintraub, Peter. "Critical Days in Kim's Pyongyang." *Far Eastern Economic Review,* November 5, 1976.

World Council of Churches, Commission of the Churches on International Affairs. "Human Rights in the Republic of Korea." *Background Information,* Geneva, Switzerland, 1979/1.

Zagoria, Donald S. "Why We Can't Leave Korea." *New York Times Magazine,* October 2, 1977.

Index

227